WomensWords

SOULFUL WOMEN

Edited by

Heather Killingray

First published in Great Britain in 2003 by
WOMENSWORDS
Remus House, Coltsfoot Drive,
Peterborough, PE2 9JX
Telephone (01733) 898101
Fax (01733) 313524

All Rights Reserved

Copyright Contributors 2003

HB ISBN 0 75434 423 1
SB ISBN 0 75434 424 X

FOREWORD

Although we are a nation of poetry writers we are accused of not reading poetry and not buying poetry books: after many years of listening to the incessant gripes of poetry publishers, I can only assume that the books they publish, in general, are books that most people do not want to read.

Poetry should not be obscure, introverted, and as cryptic as a crossword puzzle: it is the poet's duty to reach out and embrace the world.

The world owes the poet nothing and we should not be expected to dig and delve into a rambling discourse searching for some inner meaning.

The reason we write poetry (and almost all of us do) is because we want to communicate: an ideal; an idea; or a specific feeling. Poetry is as essential in communication, as a letter; a radio; a telephone, and the main criteria for selecting the poems in this anthology is very simple: they communicate.

CONTENTS

Words	Marion Ainge	1
Waking Up To Reality (1999)	Teresa Wells	2
The Girl	Anna Jones	3
A Mother's Anguish	Glenda V Llewellyn	4
Windsong	Judy Studd	5
Women On The Hunt	Elli Bainbridge	6
A Light-Hearted Look At Sex Equality	Bertha Logie	7
A New Experience	Laura Edwards	8
Our Sleepy City	Autumn Taylor	9
My Strength, My Inspiration . . . My Mother	Jacqui Watson	10
My Loss	Tara Borg	10
20,000 Miles From Home	Kate Chuter	11
Good Advice	Susan Haywood	12
Woman	Santa Pal	12
Feelings	Margaret Meek	13
Me And Mine	Jackie Rogers	13
Let There Be . . .	Jean B Cardwell	14
Daughter	Barbara Robinson	15
An Educated Idiot	Suzanne Louise Wilmott	16
Boxing Day, December 2001	Jenny Fensom	18
Mrs	Emma Sala	18
My Feelings Of Loneliness	Thelma Anne Barton	19
Young Mother	Julie E McGuigan	20
When Ginger Came To School	Lesley A Moreton	21
Engendered	Natalie Porch	22
Anorexic	Sue Brackell	23
Bedtime	Joan M Hayward	24
Irrational Fear	Kimberly Harries	24
My Mother And Me	Diane Murphy	25
Red Letter Day	Maureen Arnold	26
Tears Of Crystal	Cheryl Jackson	26
Trolley Dolly	Grace Harding	27
Forty Years On	Myra Bowen	28
Moving On	Shirley Leskiw	29

A Message To My Sisters	Amanda Eade	30
The Time	Julie Fisher	31
The Good Old Days	Joyce Kemp	32
A Call For Help	Gillian Doris Clarke	33
The Wedding	Ann E Oliphant	34
My Wish	Lorraine Allan	34
Mums	Sarah Fronte	35
Boo	Elizabeth Purdue	35
Breaking Free	Lisa Petipher	36
Dot	Ros Kane	37
Reflections	Valerie J Brickley	38
True Blue	Tracie Hammond	38
Trelos	Emma Russell	39
The Housewife's Frustration	Lyn Carter	40
More Thoughts	Irene Germain	40
Connor-James	Katie Stratton	41
Sit With Me	Katie McArevey	42
Untitled	Kim Quinn	42
Sandy Lies	Annabelle Lilly	43
The Main Thing To Remember Is . . . Relax!	Nicole Tomlin	44
Aspects Of Woman	Maura Malone	45
Coping	E Marcia Higgins	45
A Woman's Joy	J L Nowak`	46
Ode To Men	June Melbourn	47
Memories Of Home	Sarah Nicholson	48
Freedom	Georgia B Jones	48
Waiting Room	J M Miller	49
Oh No!	Farah Mirza	50
Sienna	Susan Jenkinson	50
Stupid Questions	Joanne Lilly James	51
Moonchild	Dawn Wesselby	52
Another Me	Janet Glew	52
Parting . . .	Beryl Clark	53
Hope	Helen Walker	53
A Lesson With James	C A Keohane-Johnson	54
Who Am I?	Millicent Stewart	55
To What End	J Adams	56

Through The Looking Glass	Ann-Marie Baker	56
I Am . . .	Louise Bartlett	57
The Mirror	Catherine Maguire	58
Death By Housework	Danielle Sensier	58
Criccieth Bay	Karen Brierley	59
From Mum	Alexandria Phipps	60
Old Age	Barbara Andrews	61
Cannon Fodder	Meg Wilson	62
Secrets Dreamer	Diana Rae Harding	62
Answers By A Mirror	Angela C Taylor	63
The Salad Of The Bad Café	Pamela Bakker	64
Breaking The Barrier	Eve Carter	65
Understand Me	Debbie South	66
All Over Again!	Emma Jayne Barker	66
An Ordinary Housewife	Angela Soper-Dyer	67
Why?	Eleanor Dunn	68
Who Needs A Man?	Annmarie	69
Freedom	Angel Hart	70
Nightmare	Jo Hannon	70
Spirit	Wanda Round	71
Wooden Mares	Jacquie Wyatt	72
A Woman For All Seasons	Erica Wishart	73
Untitled	Sophie Lianne Perkins	74
Sexual Delight	Jennifer Cook	74
Who Am I?	Dawn Fox	75
After The Love	Hattie Boulding	75
Let's Do Lunch	K MacCormack	76
The Big 'C'	Gill Casey	76
Toss Pot	Angie Hennigan	77
Ruth	W Rennison	77
The Heavens Wept	Maggie Connolly	78
Mother	J Good	79
Bulimia	F Buliciri	80
Honey	Kathy Rawstron	81
Blood Type	Laura S Green	82
Lost In Time	Joyce Macdonald	82
Playing Games	Nicola Newton	83
When I Was Little	Margaret Turrell	84

Looking Back On Girl Guides	Julia Owen	85
Impact	Rona Laycock	86
Is It Me?	Carolyn McCulloch	87
City 8am	Michelle Borrett	88
Two Seasons	Lorna Ledger	88
JJ	Sarah Moore	89
Cut Off Your Ears	Sharron Hollingsworth	90
Fear . . .	Sue Bentley	90
Twisted Image	Trisha Porter	91
I Know How It Feels	Christine M Wilkinson	92
Food For Thought	M Connelley	93
R	Deborah Coltman	94
Pale Pink Cardigan	Cynthia Browne	95
Me Myself . . .	Liz Osmond	96
Cameo	Eleanor Hamilton	97
Fool's Gold	Andrea Chapman	98
Limbo	Valerie Spiers	98
Choose	Gayna Florence Perry	99
The Tramp	Angela Severn	100
Not Even Love	Wendy George	101
Gather Round, My Sisters	Jo Stott	102
What About M.E?	Ruth Cottis	102
Time Of Life	James Swindlehurst	103
Dot's Old Shed	Beverley Rees	104
Disappointment	May-Tyra Tirén	104
Weighing Up The Seasons	Betty M Bennett	105
Blue Days	Luthien Lark	106
The Room	Phyllis Yeoman	107
Winter	Chaoxter Reeves	108
The Sibling	Jill Foster	108
Body Heat	Valerie Hockaday	109
Inner Voice	Kate Cowan	109
Homeless	Amy Zeglicki	110
How Good It Would Be If You Were Still Here	Cathy A Gormley-Belle	111
Found Out	Moira Jean Clelland	112
Window Shopping	Jill Fletcher	112
Acceptance	Dawn Elaine Corner	113

Solitude	Florence M Vass	114
First Kiss	Sheena Zeglicki	115
Manchester To Cornwall	Jane Colwell	116
Only A Woman Knows	Jane Winney	117
Anniversary	Jo Lee	118
Lifeline From Mother Ship	June Drysdale	119
The Lovers	Susan Harwood	120
Strategy Meeting	Sharon Leaver	120
Solitude	Sarah Margaret Munro	121
Mum's Hands	Joyce Maud Carter	121
The Dance Of Life	Gaynor Dawn Coleman	122
How Lucky I Am!	Sandra Kinnear	122
Restless	Helen Looker	123
You Are What . . .	Regine Seely	124
Love Of Life	Sylvia Ash	124
Birthday	Irene Smith	125
Snapshot	Jose Kent	126
Tiamo Sempre	Carla Lobina	127
Thoughts Of A Mum	Iris M Burgess	128
End Of An Era	Maureen Leveridge	128
Melting Moments	Linda Knight	129
Remembering Nan	Kim Thomas	130
Decided	Rose Childs	131
With You	Amber Jane Fossey	132
Platitudes	Dee Wilson	132
Merlot Fog	Ruth Belton	133
Message Of Love	Patricia M Whitehead	133
The Daydream	Anthea Bramley	134
Women's Progress	Margaret Adkin	135
My Love	Naomi Sheming	136
The Mask	Kay Chester	136
The Separation	Annette King	137
My Day	Olive M Stout	138
The Fat	Kiechelle Degale	139
Isolation	J Conium	140
Motherhood	Muriel Grey	140
A Summer's Afternoon	Margaret Brown	141
Untitled	Gaye Jowett	141

A Big Reminder	Rosemary Ward-Jackson	142
Average	Sarah Murkin	143
From My Bedroom	Marla Mitchell Coronel	144
My Teeth	Elizabeth Stevens	145
What's A Mother For?	Margaret Davies	146
Missing You	Wendy Jane Langton	146
What A Silly Statistic	Judith Gillham	147
Peace Of Mind	Jean Walker	148
Men	Patricia Thirlby	149
Mummy... Where Did I Come From?	Linda Billington	150
Remembering	Micky-Ives	151
Freedom	Jennifer Walsh	152
Old Age	C Bartholomew	152
First Hour	A A Brown	153
Until You	Michelle Penny	153
Offspring	Gloria Courts	154
Jigsaw Woman	Anna K V Hallam	154
All Of Time	Shèle K Martin	155
Alone Home	Lorna M Gough	156
Non-Sexist	Norma Rudge	157
Hopefully Out Of The Tears Comes A Smile	Maggie Lakin	158
The Final Curtain	Irene H Gabriel	159
A Woman's World	Andrea K Ellis	160
Isabel	Kathleen McGuinness	160
Loneliness	Glenda Melluish	161
I Must Get A Body	Senga Wallace Roche	162
Older Woman Driver	Judith M Warrington	163
Time To Let Go	Margaret Longcake	164
Why Do You Look At Me Like That?	Catherine Taylor	164
A Carer's Cry	Rita E Lewis	165
Opening Day At Gunwharf Quays	Gill Coombes	166
Happy Ever After	Sally Yeomans	167
Alone In The Large, Cold Bathroom	Marie-Louise McCormick	168

Title	Author	Page
Separation	Pauline Scrivener	168
An Ode To Motherhood	Sue Lowe	169
Most Things Are Rotten	Jessica Moody	170
Mum	Beth Windsor	171
My Mother	Charmaine Edwards	172
Kisses	Carol S Fenelon	173
Cardboard City	E M Clowes	174
Untitled	Elizabeth M Pritchard	174
Bitter Winds	Runa Begum	175
Schedules	Margaret Paxton	176
All These Years On . . .	Jill Gunter	177
Moving On	Rosemary Sheehan	178
Untitled . . .	Donna Drew	178
A Round Tuit	Jean Nutt	179
Love Frees	Gina Bowman	180
Holiday In Korea	Violet Beattie	180
Butterfly	Judy Studd	181
Give It Time	Maria Cope	182
This Woman's Life	Jo Hodson	182
Go Quietly	Peggy Millie Allan	183
Pretence	Elaine Rogers	184
My Privilege	M E Roberts	185
Golden Years	Audrey Haggerty	186
Single Mother	Claudia Thompson	186
Memory Box	Carly Hughes	187
Thoughts	Janet Tolliday	188
Alone We Stand	Melanie Trinder	188
The It Girl	Elizabeth Fletcher	189
Dream On!	Trudy Moss-Pearce	190
My Teenager's Room	Margaret Stanley	190
Lucy	Felicity Du Valle	191
She-Wolf	Caroline Hodgson	191
Hope	Zena Samuels	192
Butterflies	Natasha Davies	193
A Child's Cry - A Mother's Nightmare	Margaret Colville	194
A Woman	June Holmes	194
Growth And Decay	Mairead Macbeath	195

Love Is	Hilda Humphries	195
Entirely By Woman	Elva Skelton	196
The Ninth Month	Heather J Allsopp	197
A Bed	Muriel E MacKay	198
How My Life Has Changed	June Toms	199
You	Rachael Parker	200
Loving You From Afar	Paula Snowdon	200
Untitled	L Buxton	201
Omelette Metaphor Scrambled (Haiku)	Rebecca Hayward	201
Love Poem I	Margaret Bennett	202
Papa Freud's Pieta	Gisela Hoyle	203

WORDS

It was the words that hurt,
Unspoken, unsaid,
As I lay in the dark
With you, in our bed.
And I could not speak
Of what I'd read.

It was the words that hurt,
They intruded my brain.
I repeated them silently
Over again,
And learned like a child
The unwelcome refrain.

It was the words that hurt,
I should never have seen
Your private thoughts,
Your secret dream.
I scarce dare imagine
What they might mean.

It was the words that hurt,
I'll never forget
The pretence of not knowing,
The play and the set.
My performance was good,
Leading lady, but well . . .
Second best.

Marion Ainge

WAKING UP TO REALITY (1999)

I can't believe I loved you this long
I was wrong
I can't believe I put up with you
So what's new?
Nine years wasted and all those unwanted weeks
Lying to myself
As I sit on the shelf
I hate myself for being a fool, I could kick myself
Right through the wall, I've finally realised *he*
Played a game.
I hold my head in shame
I walk the streets with my head down
You made my life a circus clown, I feel so ashamed
I fell for the lie, I feel so degraded I could easily die
And still you laughed at me
You've finally wiped your feet on me
Are you sure?
No more clicky fingers wanting more
Go away you waste of space, the halo has now
Fallen around your face
I'll see your place
For nine long hears I hoped I could
For nine long years the games I've stood
After nine long years I thought you would stop laughing . . .
Please help me Lord to ease the pain
And start my life all over again
Please help me Lord, I need a new heart
I can't stand this mess I need a new start
Far away from here
Far away from here
I feel so trapped I can't get out
Nobody hears, I begin to shout
I wave a white flag, but nobody saw
I throw myself to the floor, I walk through
An invisible door to freedom

Freedom it is, freedom I'll get
Even though it's not over yet
I'll rescue myself, I'll rescue my soul
I'll save myself from this hole
No more tears for me to cry
I'm thoroughly left completely dry
You've taken my life for an easy ride
But the grass grows greener on the other side
I'll get to the stage where I'll come up on top
With my bed full of roses from an expensive shop
I'll cry my tears but not of sorrow
My time will come and I hope it's tomorrow.

Teresa Wells

THE GIRL

Like the homeless on street corners
She was the girl no one saw.
'Abused, neglected, chronic personality disorder,'
They pigeon-holed, patronised,
Passed by on the other side.
Raped, terrified, suicidal -
'A classic picture of the downhill spiral,'
But the child became a keyhole
Through which she glimpsed life.
Those innocent eyes looked
And did not turn away,
Saw no outcast, reject - only love;
And she grew under that steady gaze -
Now householder, parent,
A mother at the school gates,
A person.

Anna Jones

A Mother's Anguish

Oh daughter of mine that was once so dear
Why are we no longer so near?
I've loved you more than words can tell
So why now make my life such hell?

As a child that was so cute and bright
You kept me awake many a night.
I held you then, close to my breast
As we tried, together, to get some rest.

I loved both my children - I had two
So proud I was of both of you.
I know I pushed you both a little
That was because you were so brittle.

We have been through a lot together,
That's why I thought we meant more to each other.
We've fallen out a lot in the past,
But luckily for me it did not long last.

So thus, my child, whom I so adore,
Please do not hurt me any more.
I feel as if my life is ending,
When now it should be a happy beginning.

If you think that I'm dictating,
It's only because my heart is breaking.
My heart is so filled with terror
As I watch you make this awful error.

Just think my dear of all, and more
That we have struggled through before.
I only hope that you may find
That when with me you have peace of mind.

So I beg of thee, my daughter dear,
Please let me show you a passage clear.
You've inspired me to write in verse -
I pray to God we can yet converse.

Glenda V Llewellyn

WINDSONG

Cobwebs of confusion clear
Warm weather for heavy hearts
But the song that comes through the swirling trees
When the wild wind is raging, lighting striking
Stirs the spirit of the younger creatures
Who sing with the sighing symphony
And dance to the beat of a different drum
Who walk in a veil of tears

Winter wind wipes away the sensual
Song of summer
In the restless test of ticking time
And a gun-leaden sky several shades of grey
The wind is a whisper of secrets supreme
And wild stirrings start in my secret soul
With the ceaseless patter of falling rain
And the rumble of a distant train
The thunderclap clouds forming
But the westerly wind is still soughing
In the trembling trees
Soon to be softened by a gentler breeze
Speaking secrets in the depth of my soul
Cobwebs of confusion clear
In the garden of my heart, I hear
A stronger voice
Than the wind whispering.

Judy Studd

WOMEN ON THE HUNT

I thought I'd found a soulmate
He texted me all the time
Way into the night we chatted on line
Everything was fine

Weekends away
Weekends at home
Passionate nights
We both seemed so right

He wanted me, he wanted her
She pushed in more and more
Less time for me
No texts, no chat
I can't see me putting up with that

Second best's no good for me
I kicked him into touch
Moved on in life
I can stay free
I don't want too much

I use my men as they use me
We women of the net
A man's world it used to be
We women now stay free

Use them and abuse them
Take everything we want
It's time the tables turned
Now it's women on the hunt

Elli Bainbridge

A LIGHT-HEARTED LOOK AT SEX EQUALITY

Times are changing rapidly
Of that there is no doubt
They talk of sex equality
Let's sort this issue out.

Somewhere in the passing years
It's been the current trend
That women seldom reach the heights
Which only men attained.

But let's give this a little thought
And take a look around
There are not many places
Where no female can be found.

In factories, in transport
In every walk of life
In cleaning jobs and Parliament
You'll find the little wife.

Perhaps she is a 'Mrs'
With a settled family home
A friend, a pal, a partner
Or just choose to live alone.

Whether mother, aunt or sister
The male will always find
We're out ahead in everything
And men are way behind.

Bertha Logie

A New Experience

I like to get around and dance the night away,
Expect to be escorted about town by day.

The arrangement suited us and so succeeded -
It worked well for each was what the other needed.

Understanding that distraction was being sought
To tide us over; in the end would come to naught.

It was simply a phase through which we were going,
My toy-boy and I were a few oats out sowing.

I was compensating for the years moving on
And quite confident I was doing him no wrong.

He sought experience with one older in years,
A boost to his ego in the eyes of his peers.

It was a love unlike any others I had known,
But so pleasing, into it I had easily grown.

For I had chosen well. He was a youth of taste,
Not overbearing, arrogant, never in haste.

I shall miss him when the time comes for us to part,
And he seeks someone else closer to his heart,

By then I'll be keen to carry on again,
While of him most cherished memories will remain,

For the day I met him was I believe fateful,
He changed me so radically I am most grateful.

He activated me for another run,
Showed me that while there's life, there is a chance of fun.

The inhibitions vanished as I grew bolder,
Life really does begin at 40 or older,

For if men sport with girls on reaching middle age,
Why should toy-boys for women not become the rage?

Mine has given me a new lease of life and joy,
So I'll forever be grateful to my toy-boy.

Laura Edwards

OUR SLEEPY CITY

As darkness fell on the sleepy city
The moon only appeared through the dark skies
Children tucked up in soft, warm beds
The sound of a door banging on the shed
Only the cat can be seen
Walking along the high brick wall
Or the sound of light rain hitting the windowpane
Yet the night was just beginning
It came very quickly
The streetlights are different at night
In the city street
They seem to give a glow of their own
Shops seem to be put to sleep
And locked up tight for the night
Yet clubs and pubs come alive
With the loud music
Yet tomorrow is another day
Things will look different
And shops, pubs and clubs will still be open
Rubbish and leaves cover the streets
And homeless people begging in shop doorways
For food or loose change in the cold rain
People pass them by
And say to each other, how rude
Yet everyone lives in our so-called sleepy city.

Autumn Taylor

MY STRENGTH, MY INSPIRATION . . . MY MOTHER

For always being there, being strong
From my first steps you have supported me and given me strength
For all the sleepless nights and the tears you must have shed
worrying about me whilst I was sick
But you never showed it, knowing I was scared enough,
you stayed strong for both of us
For everything you have gone without over the years,
you never complained
For always being proud of me, helping me to believe in myself
when nobody else did
Proving to me I could achieve anything if I worked hard enough
For being my best friend, my sister and my mother
My shoulder to cry on and always making me smile again
And somehow seeing a funny side of life when it goes wrong
For never failing to amaze me and others around you
With your courage and determination to get through whatever
life throws at you
Still smiling and proud so that nobody can see the pain you are hiding
For all these things and much more
I thank you for making me the woman I am today
I only hope that if I strive hard enough I can be half the woman you are
You are and always will be my strength and inspiration . . .
My mother.

Jacqui Watson

MY LOSS

Just listen to the silence of my tears falling,
they grow louder as the days pass me by.
This house is a house, but it will no longer be a home,
as I sit in my room and cry.
I stare out of the window to watch the moon go
behind the clouds, as if to hide his face and cry.

Can it be that he can see my pain
when I hide it from the world so well?
Did you ever know the days so long,
or the nights so uninviting?
They tell me in time my hurting will heal,
but somehow I can't find the time.

Tara Borg

20,000 MILES FROM HOME

Lying next to you.
Horizontal to you, yet no symmetry unites us.
I lie here with all thoughts bundled up,
Unwrapping themselves within.
These are words you will not hear,
Although they've been screaming within me for years.

What makes you special is what's kept me silent for so long.
I've come so far to tell you,
But more than miles have I travelled
To get the answer,
Which I knew all along.

Although it makes me happy to see you're doing so well,
It's hard for me to see you can exist without me.
I came to apologise and explain myself,
But I only left with my doubts as reality,
For what I thought wasn't so.

God just doesn't want some things to be,
But that doesn't mean I don't want it for myself.
Even though I don't have the whole picture,
I have a dream,
And I want, who I want to be, in it.

Kate Chuter

GOOD ADVICE

There's plenty more fish in the sea, they say,
And pebbles on beaches abound,
For those who are single,
There's masses of shingle,
(But good men are thin on the ground!)
If I were a skate,
I'd soon find a mate,
We'd no doubt spend all our time kissing;
But sitting alone,
Communing with stone,
I just feel that something is missing . . .
The answer must be
To go hug a tree,
Dependable, solid and strong;
I think you will find,
Complete peace of mind,
But there again, I could be wrong!

Susan Haywood

WOMAN

Woman is the main part of the society,
As she has to do many works in variety.
Sometimes she's friend and at times wife and mother,
Her smiling face makes happy all others.
Her love, care and affection make the family living happily,
So she's praised by all very highly.
She ever has patience, tolerance and adjustment -
Everybody enjoys her with merriment.
A child's character always depends on her,
So she should be respected by all near and far.

Santa Pal

FEELINGS

The appointments I keep
But I don't want to speak,
When I go for a session
To cure my depression,
Demons of the past
Must be outcast.
I'm sure I'll fall flat,
I cannot do that!
I sit there and frown
Or talk myself down,
I feel in a fix
As we tend not to mix,
I need a bit of motivation,
Something that would cause sensation,
We have talents galore
And should create a furore,
Let's make it our resolution
To be part of social inclusion!

Margaret Meek

ME AND MINE

To shop, to cook, to bake
To clean, to polish, to wash
To hoover, to iron, to cry
To laugh, to shout, to weep
To hug, to scold, to love
To be, what joy.

Jackie Rogers

LET THERE BE...

P erhaps if *they* didn't have so much
E very one could have some more
A nd if *she'd* cut the gossip down
C hance is feeling would be less sore
E *very one* who's at the top should

O ffer more to share
N ot keep it all - and more - to self

E nding in, 'It's just not fair.'
A ll *those people* in the wrong! Yet
R ight seems on *their* side - while
T he like of us who do our best . . . are
H urt, blamed - with broken pride!

L *ess than truthful* seems to win, pursue them
E ven sue.
T he decent act, the kindly deed - it seems

I s overdue. But . . . it's easy
T o blame others and feel

B alm on conscience pricked. It's
E asy to look all around. Feel
G uilt-free? No! Self-tricked!
I f there's to be a better world
N o wars. No hate. Just peace.

W here can we start? What can we do?
I do believe release . . . will only be
T he strong desire of each and every person
H uman nature set aside - each

M ake a special version . . . of
'IE t it begin with me.
    That's one way that I can see'

Jean B Cardwell

DAUGHTER

Twenty years passed in an afternoon,
In your teens I would talk with you,
Tell you my thoughts,
And things to know
Give you ideas
To hang onto.

Life passed our way,
Yours and mine,
We absorbed the years,
Paths divided,
Yet stayed on a line,
A course running true.
Do you recall my words to you?
'In the whole wide world,
Only one or two,
Are really close, and deeply care
Those of a kind, your troubles share'.

Time flies, youth moves on,
Now there's a 'present',
That 'past' is gone.
Still remains a closeness,
A bond,
Sometimes grasp it,
At times feel its loss,
Yet deeply down know,
We can sift and find,
The good brought forward,
The dross left behind.

Barbara Robinson

AN EDUCATED IDIOT
(For Tracy and Dylan)

And, suddenly, you weren't seven any more.
Still short, redheaded and as big as a house
I pointed a critical finger.
You laughed, saying, 'It's a baby o' course

Whit else would it be?'

                      I struggled with the concept of you
                                      A grown up
                                        A woman
                              A mother, and couldn't.

So I shambled along after you: too much jewellery,
Woody Allen glasses, book crushed to my chest
Tongue-tied and sensible head talking about
How maybe it would be best.

To give it away.
                                        You chuckled at me
                                        Infuriating bitch!
                                              Silly cow!
                                    Stupid tart! 'It's a *baby*.'

I lectured you on the stigma of single mothers
You're economic situation (you didn't have one)
Forget about a decent job, plus the fact
You'd never get to have any fun

For the next 18 years, maybe never.
                                    You decided I worried too much
                                            Have a drink
                                             Have a fag
                                    'It's a baby, nae a bomb.'

I maintained you were mentally ill equipped
Just another teenage girl knocked up
I bemoaned and wailed this tragedy, my friend
A statistic, intellectually stuck in a rut
I *knew*, because I had done Women's Studies.

> You announced I read too much
> I was brainwashed
> Too caught up in societal norms
> You made me tea

And told me, 'ah couldna see the woods
For the trees.
Make yersel' useful an' knit some bootees or a hat.'

But I deemed myself too intellectual to knit
I stressed instead
Of the disaster that had befallen upon you
How your future was officially dead

And gone, forever.

And, suddenly, you weren't pregnant any more.
He was born, minute, crumpled, redhead
My clumsy, inept hands trembled as I held him
Then I said,
'It's a baby, Tracy,' and cried.

> I am an educated idiot.
> I understand now what you meant.

Suzanne Louise Wilmott

BOXING DAY, DECEMBER 2001

Exmouth front on Boxing Day
Folk milling everywhere
Toddlers on their Christmas trikes
Great Grandma in her chair.

Greedy gulls devouring crusts from the paths
Ritual swimmers showering in the local baths
Teenage friends chatting close
Leashed dogs straining to be free
While young lovers stand hand in hand
Watching distant sails on the sea.

The westerly wind is changing
Shoulders begin to hunch
Woollen scarves and gloves pull on
It's time to think of lunch.
People start to head for home
It's been pleasant by the sea,
'Yes we *are* calling on Aunt Maud
She's expecting us all for tea.'

Then on to the in-laws for a buffet lunch
'No, we're not stopping the night!'
You can bet your life on Boxing Day
It'll start and end in a fight!

Jenny Fensom

MRS

I wish I'd chosen not to be
The appendage to someone else's life:
Her indoors
The little woman
The old nag
The wife.

I wish I'd chosen to remain
Quite faithful to who I learnt to be:
The first born
The daughter
The successor;
The heiress of the blood which flows through me.

Emma Sala

MY FEELINGS OF LONELINESS

Loneliness becomes a part of life
That comes to many I *know*
It's a feeling of great sadness
And not easy to let *go*

It could be of someone who is in an old people's home
Who smiles at you when you open their *door*
A few words, a smile, some memories shared
To feel alone when you are there no *more*

It's of someone you know whose health and sight is not good
If only you could help and a cure could be *found*
It's isolation you feel of not hearing too good
Even though you have so many people *around*

Laughter can sometimes hide the tears that you feel
A false hope that things are *well*
Then there is someone who knows the real you
They are the only ones who can *tell*

This feeling of loneliness is hard to accept
Hoping one day it will go I will be *free*
This poem is about someone I know and it's true
This poem of loneliness is *me*

Thelma Anne Barton

YOUNG MOTHER

I'm sure she waits patiently for the moment her day dies,
when she lays herself down, closes her eyes, she's alone and she cries.
No one said it would be easy, being a mother at sixteen,
when her dreams are a constant reminder of all she could have been.
She daren't wish for anything more in the busy of her day,
for nothing compares to a mother's love for a child,
isn't that what they say?

What is wrong with me, no maternal instincts as yet?
My only instinct is to live life so to die without regret.
To grab hold of each second as if it's my last that's free,
to embrace each opportunity to let the child out inside of me.

Did she know she'd lose herself the minute she'd conceive?
Did she have time to say goodbye, to stop and grieve?
Had she planned to ever compromise herself for another?
But now that she has one, should the sister have a brother?
In her council flat with two or three, will she think she's just a mum?
Knee-deep in dirty nappies, will she despise what she's become?

My heart sinks each time she struggles by,
pushing her pram, shopping bags underneath, still in her school tie.
Is it selfish of me to want more from my life?
Not just to be remembered as someone's mother, someone's wife.

I want to be remembered as someone who went somewhere,
however, is it then that I'll regret no one is standing there?
I want to be everything that I can be until my time is through,
but is there any point, if there's no one there to tell my stories to?

And what will become of the young mother when it is her time to go?
No doubt her children will be there, with grandchildren in tow.
And how will they feel when that time has come?
I'm sure they will say 'she was a wonderful mum'.

So ask me will I regret giving up on love for success?
As I lay myself down, close my eyes for the last time, I'm alone
and my answer is yes.

Julie E McGuigan

WHEN GINGER CAME TO SCHOOL

Twelve months ago to our school came,
A little teddy bear and Ginger was her name.
She invited the children to meet with her each week.
To sit with, and listen to one another speak.
She encouraged them to be polite to each other,
With help from her dad, her mum and her brother.
She taught them how to play fun games,
To be helpful and kind, not to call each other names.
She asked them always to wait their turn,
To sit down quietly if they wanted to learn.
She talked about what made us happy or sad,
To understand our feelings, both good and bad.
The children enjoyed being Ginger's friend
And were all so upset when it came to an end.
Ginger was such a success, she now has two groups to run.
Now twice as many children can join in with the fun!

Lesley A Moreton

ENGENDERED

Bright and dewy was the morning when eternity began -
When we drew our lot and the one I got was 'Company for Man',
A pretty slave to clean his cave and populate his Earth,
'What joy!' I cried as I was tied to endless giving birth.

For hours I had generations suckled to my breast,
And soon my mind felt disinclined to feign an interest,
My companion hunted, grunted, had me in his den - which meant
I'd covered several continents by nigh on half-past ten.

By midday Man was cultured and had found the time to think,
He invented himself a war machine and me a kitchen sink,
He conquered distant kingdoms and destroyed them block by block,
He had me call him 'my good sir', while smiling in a frock.

Through all I acted perfectly; congenial, polite,
But in the shadows of late afternoon Man hid me out of sight.
The monotony was hell for me, I had to sew for leisure,
Converse in trivialities and be grateful for the pleasure!

Well I rebelled, I felt compelled and what a sweet relief
As I indulged emerging sassiness not within my brief,
At evening tide I set aside some time to spread the word -
'Man is ruffled by the feathers of this bright new breed of bird'.

I swapped my rags for shoulder pads and Sonny Jim took note,
I clawed back debts with interest and swiped the right to vote.
I controlled his empires for amusement and delight,
I bought and sold, I broke the mould, I wore the trousers out of spite.

And yet all this failed to satisfy the driving need in me, you see -
I wanted not his lot in life, just my identity.
All those hours wasted, midnight before I knew,
Man or Woman - doesn't matter, it's not what we are but who.

Natalie Porch

ANOREXIC

The morning you were born
Dawn chorus sang.
I cradled your sweet shape to me.
Your skin, tinged gentle pink,
Not scarlet or vermilion, clung close to mine.
I loved your foetal form, curled in my arms,
Ready to unfurl, unfold,
Like some small sea-flower
Or tiny cherub in a shell.

A dozen years on
I hold your still-sweet shape to me.
Though now cadaverous,
Emaciated, gaunt,
With jutting rib-cage and starved, sunken eyes,
I love your skeletal form,
Your icy hands and ivory face.
And how I yearn to comfort you,
Breathe warmth into your veins,
Breathe flesh onto your bones,
Breathe life into your limbs,
As if my love could suddenly arrest
This terrible decay,
This cruel and cankerous malignancy
Which ravenously feeds upon your fragile form,
This slow attenuation
Of your small, shrunken frame,
So savagely devoured and gorged upon,
This flickering and fading,
Faltering, inexorable
Dwindling away . . .

Sue Brackell

BEDTIME

His mother gave it to us when we wed, a four-foot-six double bed.
In it we lay and loved and planned, and life seemed grand.
We did not care if each did not get a share of blanket or sheet . . .
Until the pleasure turned to strain.
He could not bear the babies' cries each night.
It was plain that we would have to separate.
So he slept in the small back room while I sat in gloom
In that wide bed and each baby fed.
But one year in anger cold I bought divans and sold that bed.
The children weep, no longer can they creep into the warm
By my round form, for a Sunday snuggle.
And my beloved cannot rest his puzzled head on my soft breast
Until we bridge the gap that pride and that wide distance
The years has brought. So now we sleep in each chaste bed,
Or lay close and sweet in just three feet.
'I see this is a modern trend,' he said,
'But I wish you'd kept that double bed.'

The decades have gone, the family has fled,
We now cuddle for comfort in a new double bed.

Once again I am alone in a single bed,
Not pride, only sorrow - my beloved is dead.

Joan M Hayward

IRRATIONAL FEAR

The hairs on your neck stand on end,
Your lips quiver together in silent motion,
Your eyes unmoving fixed on the same point,
You let out an escaped cry full of wretched emotion.

Despair clouds your vision,
Your mind is numb of all thoughtful insight,
Your stomach churns as if a thousand hands,
Are pushing and prodding you with all their might.

Your shoulders feel heavy and your knees weak,
As if any second you would collapse on the ground,
Bereaved shivers lapse your whole body,
You whisper a prayer, but produce no sound.

Out of the corner of your eye you see it move,
Awakened from its hollow hiding place,
As if it sensed your irrational fear,
A frivolous cry escapes your stone white face.

Kimberly Harries

MY MOTHER AND ME

She was hurting and poor
Struggling for money and couldn't take any more
With four kids under her feet
Empty bellies and needs she couldn't meet.

My mother was sad and cried a lot
Her anger and frustration bottled up like bubbling soup in a pot
I often went to my room to hide
All this unhappiness was torture for me inside.

I am one of those kids
Who grew up unhappy and sad
My mother's beliefs were all I had
Passed on to me, but I have struggled to set me free.

She couldn't work, had no self-esteem
But I've changed the pattern for me I mean
I work and study to provide for my family
My children have fun and play happily.

I have learned new ways, and new beliefs
Oh what a joy, it's such a relief
I can now teach my children to be
Happy and positive, not negative and misery.

Diane Murphy

RED LETTER DAY

I have a present for your daughter, she is lovely, isn't she?
Please don't ask him in Mum, keep him away from me!
She calls me to say thank you, he bends to give me a kiss,
I turn away from him to make certain he will miss,
And I throw his gift back at him, it is a teddy bear,
And I go into the garden until I know he is no longer there.

When my dad comes home, I will tell him about the man next door,
And I know he will sort him out for sure.
He says no one will believe me, and that it's my fault anyway,
And that he is coming back to get me on another day.
My mum thinks he is so nice to make a fuss of me,
But she doesn't know the things he does, I wish that she could see.

Mum has just gone to get my dad and I am on my own,
He keeps knocking on the door, why won't he leave me alone?
Suddenly I hear a scuffle, then Dad walks through the door,
Don't worry Darling he says, he won't come back any more.
Police came and everything, then they took him away,
That's the day my life began, a real red letter day.

Maureen Arnold

TEARS OF CRYSTAL

Heated breath condense and fall,
Against the mirror on the wall,
Through crystal droplets multiplied,
Look inside,
Enjoy the ride,
Blazing bodies clang, clash, collide.

Within its frame we replicate,
Erotic desires that penetrate,
The most sinister realms of the mortal's mind,
To human shame we are no longer blind.

The image is glossy, shiny and bold,
As we see a sexual stance unfold,
But the true beauty remains untold,
Even though the soul is something you cannot hold,
So cruel to leave it feeling so cold.

Cheryl Jackson

TROLLEY DOLLY

A rainy day, the traffic is bad,
A honking of horns as drivers grow mad!
Will I be able to park
Before it gets too dark?
There's an empty space in sight
Over which two young women fight.
Please let me find an empty bay,
Oh, please God help me, I pray.
At last I've parked and am through the door,
But, oh dear me, what a crowded store!
My trolley will not go the way I wish,
The wheels turn to the meat instead of the fish!
Shopping completed, I go to the till
Searching for my purse to pay the bill.
I thought I'd chosen the shortest queue,
But now the cashier has gone to the loo!
Hooray, I just have the shopping to pack,
There's only half a mile tailback!
I arrive home - a cup of tea would be nice,
But, alas, I left it at the till with the rice!
Back to the supermarket I'll have to go,
And thus I end my tale of woe!

Grace Harding

FORTY YEARS ON

I long to see your face
Long to touch your brow
Children leave traces of where
They have been but you,
You left nothing but tears.

There are those who scream
That mine is a hollow dream
But I see you walking between
Your brother and your sister
Claiming your rightful ordinal position.

The likeness between them is stark
Despite the different coloured eyes.
Struggling in the wilderness
I paint your face with their shadows,
Gain some comfort from this although

The colour of your eyes escapes me
And your features remain a secret
Hidden inside the tunnel of the past,
But the hair, that has to be golden,
Like mine, like his, like theirs.

Those about me fail to understand
Even he who is closest to me
Offers little comfort but a wintry smile.
Sixteen weeks? Never, ever existed.
A four month foetus is a nothing.

You remain the lost one
Whom I yearn to caress
You were my precious little one.
Forty years on and still the ache
Rests heavily across my breast but one day, one day . . .

Myra Bowen

MOVING ON

The house is empty
The rooms are bare
Into the corners
I stand and stare

I should be happy
I'm moving at last
But now I feel sad
It's all happened so fast

So much has happened
In this house of mine
But give me a few days
And I'll be fine

I check the rooms
Make sure everything's gone
I count the stairs
I've lived here too long

So to each room
I say goodbye
I know I'll be happy
I'm not going to cry

I lock the doors
And walk away
This is the beginning
Of a brand new day.

Shirley Leskiw

A Message To My Sisters

Carried along on the wave of life
Not a moment to stop, to think
No time for wonders; aspirations
A little dream only after a drink

Riding the storms of debts and bills
Mortgage, traffic and queues
Waiting for that rosy day in the future
The day that will never ensue

House buying, marriage, a dog then some kids
Nappies, teenagers, weddings, more kids

And hence, we are lost in the seas of life
'Til the waters of youth ebb away
Suddenly we are old and pained
Wrinkled, grumpy and grey

Therefore, take heed my preoccupied friends
Lest the waves carry too fast
Make time to reflect and relish your life
Make the good times and happiness last

Never forget who you are, what you dreamed
Never forget yourself *you*
Don't ever think I can't or I don't
Only I can! Or I do!

Be happy, fulfilling your every dream
Fill every day knowing it is a gift
Even then you'll get old and wrinkly and grey
But at least you will feel that you've *lived*

Amanda Eade

THE TIME

I saw the clock's face as I turned from yours
Heard my voice, pure molten fury
You lay beside me, still and silent
The baby boiled inside me
As I raged to find out why
You were no longer you

I saw the clock's face as I turned from yours
'You must have someone else'
So many times denied
A beat
Then six words pierced my soul
And the pain erupted

I saw the clock's face as I turned from yours
'I didn't want you to know'
Course not, you wanted both lives
Greed, greed, greed
Now you must choose
Wife and child or painted mistress

I saw the clock's face as I turned from yours
As I would see it hour upon hour
On so many long and tortured nights
As I lay sleepless fixed on the spiteful slow hands
Waiting for your return from her
I hated that clock

I saw the clock's face as I turned from yours
And I see it still across a quarter century
Cold, gleaming stainless steel carcass
Glinting hands and intrusive purple face
So cruel
All that love, what a waste

Julie Fisher

The Good Old Days

We sat at two long benches
Our hands a blur, turning, turning,
Icing sugar squeezing, folding
Into flowers, thousands and thousands.
Piece-work concentrated the mind,
Heads bent down, getting it done,
The slow ovens filling up behind
Us, with flowers, tray after tray.
Workers' playtime, we sang along,
Housewives' choice, we sent requests.
Quoted from the latest film dialogue,
Sang whole scores from musicals.
Down from London our boss would strut
And tell of the latest vase he'd bought.
Our wages were a pittance, derisory,
No trade union to lend their support.
The floors were thick with icing and mud;
On Saturdays for an extra five bob
Two of us could volunteer to scrub.
Hygiene inspectors passed all without reproach.
We talked of our families, boyfriends, hopes,
The dance on the pier, listening to 'The Goons'.
Trips to London for a jazz concert,
Wrestling, boxing, football, told jokes,
Whispering about the latest girl in trouble,
(There was no magic pill in the fifties),
Then at last a new factory gave us hope,
A decent wage, new lives in the sixties.

Joyce Kemp

A CALL FOR HELP

I call for help, but no one hears
and all I do is cry through tears,
As each day unfolds I hope and pray
that I'm not feeling this low today,
How miserable I am, so discontent
did I know, for me, that this was meant?
For me to see to everyone's needs,
as I seem to be in the background
while they do just as they please?
I cry each day, I feel unhappy
why is my life so dull and empty?
For I aim to do what I think is best
and everyone puts my nerves to the test.
How much can I take? I do not know,
I wish that someone could tell me so
for I feel alone and somewhat glum
and what have I achieved at being a mum?
A tiny flat so sleazy, so small
living there is no fun at all
and with what my life consists of every day
there is no time for *'me'* or play!
As when my working day is done
I look into the mirror and see what I've become.
My smile has gone from upon my face
and when I frown it leaves a trace.
The frown never used to bother me . . .
. . . But lately it is there 'permanently'.

Gillian Doris Clarke

The Wedding

The church was strangely silent 'cept the organ playing low
The groom stood there before me as you did so long ago
His thoughts you could interpret by the look upon his face
'Twas love, hope and a little fear in this unfamiliar place.
It took me back to years ago - that day you made a vow
The same hopes and fears you must have felt - we're still together now
You kept those promises made at that time to me
And every day I love you, as all these things I see -
Our children happily growing up, this groom at the altar stood
Down the aisle you slowly march, as he surely hoped you would
You look the same to me as you did then - as proud as proud can be
And well you might as one who has been such a joy to me.
As the young man at the altar gives our daughter her wedding band
I silently renew our vows as you turn and clasp my hand
Let's hope that when their children reach this stage in life
This groom can turn in church and say, 'I'm glad we're man and wife.'

Ann E Oliphant

My Wish

Where sunbeams dance throughout the day
sweetest lambs gambol while children play
Where rainbows glow from up above and
days are filled with everlasting love
Where the songbird flies to pastures new and
dreams we dream always do come true
Where laughter and singing is all around and
peace and happiness forever abound
When the sun goes down at the end of the day
for all these things I kneel and pray

Lorraine Allan

MUMS

Will you ever know what it's like to be a mother?
The pain and the struggle to give life to another.
The love that hits you as soon as you see them
The worry that becomes you and the happiness you wish them.
Although at times they are such a strain
You thank God you've got them again and again.
You think of the future, wanting only the best
What will become of them when they leave the nest?
They don't know you love them or how much you do,
Or will they one day when they're parents like you?
So please understand when we go on and on,
That we are just scared of getting it wrong.
And next time you're sitting feeling sorry and forlorn,
Try to remember how we felt when you were born.

Sarah Fronte

BOO
(1975 - 1990)

She came into our hearts and lives
So small and scared with yellow eyes
A tiny grey bundle unaware
That we would show her love and care
She had to trust, she had no choice
For kittens do not have a voice
We had her almost sixteen years
She brought us joy and sometimes tears
I love her more than words can say
And will miss her now she's gone away
She could not choose her family
But I'm so pleased she came to me

Elizabeth Purdue

BREAKING FREE

A swollen lip,
A blackened eye,
I tripped and fell,
Another lie,
Hidden pain,
Lost pride and shame,
I know it will
Still happen again.
This merry-go-round
Of secrets and guilt,
I've done no wrong,
I cannot wilt.
I've 3 scared children,
Who've heard my screams.
Their frightened faces,
I see in my dreams,
I owe it to them,
To finally break free.
I know I have the strength,
To see it through,
I can see the light
I know what to do.
There's no looking back,
Forward I will move,
Hopeful at last
My wishes will prove
No more trouble and strife,
No more a battered life,
No more the battered wife.

Lisa Petipher

DOT

She's not the Woman of the House
And she grows more beautiful
With each baby

She's slight and slim
And you don't always know where she is
She's in some corner of her home
Or out of it
Doing her thing

She doesn't seem to be in charge
Yet she contains
Her children, us visitors, the cats
Quietly, with respect

She has a man, Mike, a big man,
Everyone knows Mike
But no way
Is she what big men
Are supposed to have behind them

She says what she wants
And does what she likes
I don't know if she suffers
But some sort of strength carries her along

She's not the Woman of the House
And she grows more beautiful
With each baby

Ros Kane

REFLECTIONS

I look in the mirror,
What do I see?
A patchwork quilt
The reflection of me.
I've tried all the creams
To ward off old-age
But to my dismay
I still see a page
Like the lines in a book
Staring back at me.
I'm luckier than some
I have all my hair
Just a grey streak or two
So I suppose it will do.
A touch of mascara, eye shadow too
Foundation of course
To liven the view.
Oh dear, why are you so vain?
It's not as if, you're exactly plain.
You're not too bad
When you're all dolled up.
Says me to the mirror
I think you will do
Who cares, about a line or two?

Valerie J Brickley

TRUE BLUE

As I sit down to write,
darkness covers the bright sunlight.
Sky turns purple with a shade of blue,
my heart sinks as I think of you.

Lying awake not able to sleep,
the room grows darker as a gloom starts to creep.
Through quiet and lonely times of despair,
a warm heart when I shut my eyes and see you there.

Tracie Hammond

TRELOS

Moment to moment
You won't think of me,
Rather catch my presence
In a stray curl of sunshine
Or strangers laughing in the street.
Autumn to winter
Things come to pass,
Life simply unravels
But I won't forget us
Making love through Aegean heat.
Quiet talk over strong coffee
Grappling on the beach,
Warm back and shoulders
These images I reach.
Laughing hard and clanging
Stoned and playing chess,
This is a good love pirate
Some have died for less.
What else can I say?
A writer strangely dumb,
It's all been worth it
Even when I'm under thumb.
Sometimes we berate each other
But strong feelings still remain,
I love you, I love you, I love you
May I inconvenience you again?

Emma Russell

THE HOUSEWIFE'S FRUSTRATION

Frustration speaks very loud
Misunderstood by the crowd
How can I say what I mean?
When all that's felt is so unseen
Expectation never given
Academic only driven
Natural ability if given space
Will give you chance to find your place
What about expanding the mind?
If discussions give answers nowhere to find
Expressions locked up with no escape
Me read notes? Listen to tapes!
What about interaction
Shared ideas satisfaction?
What about hopes and dreams
Shared ideals, thought out schemes?
Can't keep being a nice housewife
I want a bigger slice of life!
Chance to contribute, intelligent debate
To express my thought at a sensible rate
To grasp the issue, to have a voice
All I want is a wider choice!

Lyn Carter

MORE THOUGHTS

What is the matter with me I say
Can I not be happy again
Carefree, happy, light as a bird
Instead of solid, dull, miserable pain
What gives me joy I ask myself
Green fields, trees and the good brown earth
To grow flowers, full of colour
Vegetables that taste like no other

To hear the birds, see butterflies
To look up, and see the clear blue skies
Could it be I'm selfish, unsociable, a bore
For when I'm in company
I look at the door
I hear the jokes, the talk
The same, again, again
Let me out, let me be sane.

Irene Germain

CONNOR-JAMES

A sunny day, a bundle of joy,
Into my life a handsome baby boy,
Five fingers, five toes and a wicked smile,
You've made life so much more worthwhile.
You've filled my heart with love so true,
With all the priceless things you do,
You're learning fast, already waving goodbyes,
So now I'll teach you 'Auntie Katie' and 'hi'.
Climbing the stairs and crawling already,
Throwing your toys and cuddling your teddy.
Soon there will be lots more we can do,
Like walks in the park, riding a bike and kicking a ball too.
I'll teach you your left from your right,
We can draw and paint using colours so bright,
We can go shopping and eat McD's
With Granna, Poppa and little sister Marnie-Lee.
All these lovely things we can enjoy and share,
Bringing you up with lots of love and care,
We'll develop a bond so unique and rare,
Teaching you life's values, what's right, wrong and fair,
So little Connor-James there's lots of years to look forward to,
And through the years, no matter what Auntie Katie will always be there for you.

Katie Stratton

SIT WITH ME

Sit with me once more my love
Sit with me once more
And speak and laugh and sing and dance
Just like we've done before

Among whispering trees and whistling winds
I ache for your tune to soar
Above the birds, among the stars
Sing for me once more

Give me again those blissful words
Rock me gently through Heaven's door
Enchant my grieving tears with laughter
Speak to me once more

Leave me not alone in this quiet place
Let us dance again on this green floor
Bring me your face so these old hands may touch
Your rosy red lips once more

And if this cannot be my love
Let me join you forever more
In our starlight ballroom up above
Sit with me once more

Katie McArevey

UNTITLED

If I knew what I was lacking
If I knew just where to look
Like a floating lump of jetsam
Feeling, looking for its hook.

How can you know what's lacking
What feels so undefined
When the questions that are opened
Lay unanswered in your mind?

A piece of jigsaw's missing
One card has gone astray
Will you tell me where it's gone to
So that I might find my way?

As if I've lost my children
Or cannot locate a key
I feel a hole
This needy soul
It's me, it's me, it's me.

Kim Quinn

SANDY LIES

Another world, another day,
How long will people live this way?
I thought that I had seen it all,
But now I'm not so sure.
A woman cries, no one must notice,
In this man's world, another focus.

The elegance is astounding,
But only the privileged can capture these surroundings.
The city is wide marbled and Roman,
But this is no place for a woman.
They scuttle about their daily lives,
Shrouded in black for their disguise.

The desert is yellow, red and golden,
Only camels roam in the sun's fierce lumen.
Many creatures come out at night,
And their existence is an amazing fight.
Bedouins rule these golden planes,
Centuries away from our western games.

Annabelle Lilly

THE MAIN THING TO REMEMBER IS . . . RELAX!

'It's really not that bad.'
'Oh no! It didn't hurt me.'
'The main thing to remember is . . . relax!'
'*Relax?* - Are they completely off their trolley?'

The letter arrived yesterday. The words jumped out of the page;
Advisable, *Cervical Smear Test*, it is simple and painless,
and picks up abnormal changes in the cervix at a very early stage.

My appointment was now booked. The time had finally come.
I spent the day simply terrified! 'Oh! How I *needed* my mum!'

There was no turning back, for my own good this had to be done.
I entered the room, chatted with the nurse, clapped eyes on the utensils,
and instantly considered making a run.

Now the nurse has seen this all before, but frankly, this part I had
dread!
So I summoned up my courage, whipped off my trousers and nicks,
laid on the couch and thought . . .
Is there anything more embarrassing? - 'OK go ahead.'

As the nurse got on with her job - I *tried* to relax.
Yet with everything so tightly clenched and tense and mind
full of worry,
I made things more discomforting and so longed to scream -
This hurts! Have you found Australia? Come on! Let's hurry!

Looking back to my smear test, it *really wasn't* that bad.
Results came through, all was clear,
Phew! Am I thrilled and far more than glad!

The point is, all women should fairly regularly have this test,
and *remember* - '*relax*' is the key word here.
It only takes a few *important* minutes,
and once it's done, you can give a *great big cheer!*

Nicole Tomlin

ASPECTS OF WOMAN

Woman kind, woman blind, woman with yashmak on her face,
woman in a state of grace, woman of state, woman in a state.
Mother, daughter, mother-in-law, ha ha ha,
Auntie, girlfriend, breaking the law.

Prostitute, bleached head, painted nails, housewife bleached hands,
pots and pans.
Nose in the air, laddered tights, family fights.

Vegetable plot, plotting finance, watching the clock, tick-tock,
tick-tock.
To the station she is rushing, coughing, coping, trolley pushing.
Woman of war, dress all tore, woman on the land, sifting the sand.
Career woman, ambition gone sour, not enough power.
Inebriate woman, lost her way, cannot remember the time or day.
Woman covered from head to foot in stifling heat in a desert hut.
Strong willed woman with no regrets, looking forward, hedges her bets,
try and catch her if you can, friend of woman, loved by man.

Maura Malone

COPING

Awake, awake, it is morning and the day has begun.
This night, this terrible night, pushes me down, down
back into oblivion.
This thick, dark blanket of depression, this quilt of despair,
engulfs me, stifles me.
Far above, like stars in the heavens, are many signs,
The one reading 'happiness' is at the furthermost edge of the galaxy -
A million light years from my grasp.
I fight and struggle, please help, please help.
This daily battle - familiar now.
I break through - and clutch the sign which reads 'coping'.

E Marcia Higgins

A Woman's Joy

Life is so stressful,
Of this I must speak,
But there's nothing worse,
Than shopping for the week.

Off we all dash,
Trolleys at the ready,
Try not to clash,
Remember hold it steady!

Down the first aisle,
Slipping on floors worn like silk,
Stretching to reach yoghurts,
Come cries of, ''Ere 'ave you got any milk.'

Rushing down toiletries,
With sudden energy you burst,
As you see the last deodorant,
Elbowed by, 'Oy I was 'ere first!'

Rushing down the meat aisle,
Planning roast for the week, what joy,
As you're splattered by with a tube of Smarties,
By an squealing little boy.

A wave of relief you feel now,
Approaching the checkout, calm and wiser,
As you're then told at the till,
''Ang on I need a supervisor!'

After half an hour you're finally released
Feeling exhausted, almost asleep,
Then the dreadful truth creeps in,
You have it all to do again next week!

J L Nowak

ODE TO MEN

Men are all on power trips,
They have to be in charge,
They like to show off to the world,
Their egos are so large.

They're hopeless with the housework,
They haven't got a clue,
They take it all for granted,
Like everything you do!

They always want a meal cooked,
It saves them buying food,
If asked to be taken out one night,
They're in a right old mood.

Their driving is atrocious,
They tailgate all the time,
They scorn all women drivers,
As if they were a crime.

Watching blinking TV,
What sport is on today?
Do jobs around the garden,
Why ask, I have to say?

Jealous of our girlfriends,
Look down upon their chatter,
And when you're feeling poorly,
Whatever is the matter?

We always know where to find them,
They are never very far,
They are in the local hostelry,
Propping up the bar!

June Melbourn

MEMORIES OF HOME

Magnificent majestic mountains
Reaching for the sky
Concealing hundreds of secrets
From centuries gone by
As I stand and gaze in awe
Your splendour doth ever grow
Seasonally changing from purple heather
Golden bracken to sparkling crisp white snow
You shelter the red deer
The fox and the tiny roe
Engulfing them in gullies
Where the hunter cannot go
Beautiful cascading waterfalls
Dispersing into little streams
Often at night when I am restless
These memories haunt my dreams
Magnificent majestic mountains
Had I a magic wand
My wish would be this very hour
To be home in dear Scotland

Sarah Nicholson

FREEDOM

I have to feel free,
As the birds in the sky,
As a bee buzzing by,
I have to feel free.

I've got to be me,
Feel the wind in my hair,
With never a care,
I've got to be me.

Yet I need to be part
Of the big scheme of things,
And know in my heart
That although I have wings,
I belong.

Georgia B Jones

WAITING ROOM

Shabby grey chairs,
Haphazardly arranged.
Anti-smoking posters,
Two faded landscapes.

Pile of women's weeklies,
National Geographic.
Old Readers' Digests,
De-hydrated pot plant.

Avoiding eye contact,
Silent assembly.
Twiddling coat buttons,
Examining fingernails.

Flicking through magazines,
Without concentration.
Mental dress rehearsal,
For imminent confrontation.

Child tips out Lego,
Scattering afar.
Bright primary colours,
Jewels on the floor.

J M Miller

OH NO!

I got out of bed,
And looked in the mirror,
I saw a different person,
With spots and greasy hair,
Looking straight at me in the reflection,
I had a bad temper,
Or was it just a bad dream?
I turned around to check if anyone was there,
Tears came pouring out of my eyes,
Why had I turned so ugly overnight?
Was God punishing me for something I did wrong
Or had I caught a disease off one of the geeks?
Now I'd have to be one of them,
Oh no!
I won't be popular any more,
I wish I was a child again,
All these years I tried to act older,
How I wish I could turn back the hands of time,
And be a little younger.

Farah Mirza

SIENNA

Churning and churning
A victory sought.
The prize obsession,
Already bought.

Assassin's truth,
Will it be told?
A profitable story,
Begging to be sold.

Many, many others,
Have come before,
To this great presence,
I unlock the door.

Emptiness filling,
A satirical void,
Have we accomplished,
A satisfactory goal.

Susan Jenkinson

STUPID QUESTIONS

Life is merely a series of uneventful days
Interrupted by events.
How rude.
My mother said it was rude to interrupt,
Yet she was the one always pestering me!
Talk about hypocritical.
My teacher said I should learn,
And learn I did,
But what did I learn?
Dunno mate.
And old stinking tramp told me I was stingy,
Cos I only gave him a quid.
That was all I had!
Except for the fiver in my back pocket.
My father said I 'should get a proper job'
So I became a writer.
D' you think he's pleased?

Joanne Lilly James

MOONCHILD

I know
You are
A child of the moon
For I
Have touched
Your alabaster skin
And I
Have smelt
The scent of your sorrow
I too
Have felt
The pain you cannot heal
I wait
For petals
Of the darkest night
Only then
Can I
Hold you near to me
I am
Not afraid
Of your darkest shadow
For one day
I will
Illuminate your soul

Dawn Wesselby

ANOTHER ME

I think of my make-up as a mask
Trying to hide the real me.
Which mask will I wear tomorrow?

Janet Glew

PARTING...

A starry sky one summer's night,
- the opening of a gate,
- the gentle stirring of the trees,
- a well remembered date;
the memory is a wondrous thing,
it plays so many tricks.
When you've just lost the one you love -
your heart but barely ticks!
You have to start to cook for one,
- not two chairs, there's just me;
the washing up's done all alone,
- no fights about TV.
My heart just isn't bruised alone,
it's simply ripped in two.
They never warned me love could change,
- that you'd find someone new!
I guess I'll try to carry on
and aim to start anew;
but in my heart there'll always be
fond memories of you.

Beryl Clark

HOPE

Lost in the mists of time
Beyond passion
And disgust;
So far back
Light reaches,
Short of a grasp.

Helen Walker

A LESSON WITH JAMES
(Especially for James Richard Johnson - born 10.08.00 at 12.45pm)

I have learnt since your birth
There is nothing more precious on Earth
Than you.
I have learnt to be unselfish
Because you are everything I cherish.
I have learnt to be more grateful
Because you are perfect and beautiful.
You are my everything,
My darling.
A joy to behold
A story waiting to be told.
I have learnt that patience is a virtue
Something I never had before you.
I have learnt to appreciate life more
I never knew motherhood before.
I have learnt when you are sleeping
You are safely in my keeping.
I learn new things every day
You are developing in every way.
I have learnt to enjoy childish games
With you, my darling son, James.
I have learnt there is nothing finer that the gift of motherhood.
And if I could
Dear James, I would
Have you over and over again
No matter how great the labour pain.

C A Keohane-Johnson

WHO AM I?

Who am I?
A woman for sure, a mass of soft warm flesh
that cradles my baby, all of him comforting,
soothing, giving strength and inspiring confidence.

Who am I?
A mass of soft warm flesh, crumpling in a heap of tears
under the weight of self-induced responsibilities.
Shoulder sagging under the weight of
misconceptions and false pride.

Who am I?
Contradictions, emotions that wax and wane
with the cycles of my womanhood?
The moon, who knows?
The gentle spiritual warrior that envelopes
a lost or hurting soul.
Giving hope, full of promise, a powerful, light worker.
Illuminating the dark spaces in my psyche
if only one moment in time.

Who am I?
I am infinite possibilities, darkness and light,
weakness and strength,
whole, yet incomplete.
I am all that is, ever was, ever will be.

Millicent Stewart

To What End

The world is oh so big yet small
You do your best for one and all
The years go by so quickly now
But still you ask yourself, when and how
The sun beams down and makes you smile
But this doesn't last long, just for a while
You work all week to make ends meet
And hope the weekend will bring you a treat
You raise your family the best you can
And think back to how it all began
At this stage in life we should have no cares
But somehow it seems who wins, who dares
You lie awake until nearly dawn
Just listening for that familiar horn
Your family grown and their problems too
It takes more than a cuddle to get them through
You look at all you have achieved in life
Your home, your children and when you made me your wife
You realise that everything is on lend
And say to yourself, to what end?

J Adams

Through The Looking Glass

I do not want to pry
But what is in your eye
I see a tear of fear
I see nothing at all
I do not see life or death
I cannot see you
I cannot see me, but what can I see?
I see fear and lies

You're just a shell
There are no outer feelings
You live in a mirrored life
Within your own head
You do not see what is happening to you
You've lost your life light
You've lost your spark
You've lost yourself.

Ann-Marie Baker

I AM...

I am who I am; I'll be who I'll be.
Why should I pretend that this is not the real me?
This is my way of thinking and my way of life,
I'm not just a husband or somebody's wife.
There's more to me than meets the eye,
you will soon discover,
If you get below the surface
and don't judge me by the cover.
Learn by example, follow the crowd,
if you so desire,
but you must find out what is right for you
and what fuels your own life's fire.
Narrow-minded people are blinded by difference,
they almost see right through,
but your beliefs and truths are yours alone
and personal to you.
Just be yourself, whoever you are,
because life is a show and you are the star!

Louise Bartlett

THE MIRROR

The mirror holds an image
the person looks like me
I am a true reflection
of what you all can see.
The people that surround me
the life that is my own
I chose to be this person
the image I have sown.
But sometimes when I look
beyond the mirror's face
I see a secret life
in a different place
unfamiliar faces, places out of reach
holding hands with fantasy
on some deserted beach.
I wonder what it would be like
to leave my life's routine
and go where no one knows me
some place I've never been,
to steal away, to leave behind
and from my life be free
the mirror holds an image
but is it really me.

Catherine Maguire

DEATH BY HOUSEWORK

The kitchen was all surfaces.
Know what I mean?
Really clean.
All done and dusted, sneezes black.
The woodwork gleamed.
Stain removal, let me count the ways.
One day she'd write the book.

In the corners of the room,
clinging fiercely, cobweb strands.
Hidden fingers in a cupboard,
perish,
spreading crystal spores.
Lying down, I found her
with the laundry,
folded over, knees tucked in.

Danielle Sensier

CRICCIETH BAY

Protective mother
stands serene
offspring hidden behind her stone apron.

Husband at her feet,
daily showing affection,
his green and white salty caresses
wear her down.

Marriage on the rocks . . .
as she accepts another's presents . . .

Greasy spaghetti
Cola cans
excrement.

Gifts donated
by an interfering lover;
humanity.

Karen Brierley

FROM MUM

I tried to send you money
instead of all my love
I don't know how to reach you
since Dad moved up above

I tried to do my best for you
but Steven shone the best
I don't know how to love you
I guess you know the rest

My own life's not been rosy
but that's no real excuse
I often wonder how it might be
if we could call a truce

I sit and ponder every day
this is a very, short-lived life
to mend the rift between us
but then . . . there's Steven and his wife

I know they wouldn't like it
if you were part of me again
for they reap all the glory
and to you I give just pain

I've heard you've been quite ill of late
I guess that's just a lie
but . . . I've made no move to reach you
I guess this must be goodbye

I'd like to send you £50
because I feel so bad inside
and as I write the cheque to you
I know to myself I've lied

Goodbye to you my strong one
the weak is my concern
one day we'll meet in Heaven
and it will surely be your turn.

Alexandria Phipps

OLD AGE

In the mirror I caught a glance
what I saw made me want to shout and dance,
not with joy but with such rage
my body it's showing signs of age.
Rolls of fat in lots of places
my stomach it could do with braces,
my boobs have started to sag
why's old age such a drag.
It's no good, I'll have to slim
oh I wish that I was thin
exercises I'll do for sure
if I can get down on the floor.
I'm going to slim with such vigour
to get back some sort of figure,
if it works I might feel great
like 53 not 68.
Giving up the sweets and cakes
will power, I'm told, is all it takes,
of that I've got none at all
so I'm off to the church hall.
Slimming club once a week
of my weight I cannot speak,
I'll do my best for this body of mine
to help hold back the ravages of time.

Barbara Andrews

CANNON FODDER

Women speak of love, for they are able.
In men there is a cable
of wire. They are unable
to reveal their deepest self.
There is also a stopper,
and boy it's a whopper,
so what with wire to twist
and stoppers to stop,
no wonder men become cannon fodder.
Where will it end, this division of open,
and closed seen on every man's breast?
Aren't women blessed?
Except when they love -
then it's hard
to find just a shard.
The remains of the cannon fodder,
and wonder - oh God, is that all?

Meg Wilson

SECRETS DREAMER

I search for you
I see you everywhere
In my dreams I kiss your eyelashes
When we meet I hold your gaze
Are we players' truth or dare?

My spirit soars like spinning dolphins
Lost in my dreams of our first embrace
Where our lips brush feathered kisses
Trembling, falling into one another
It's only seconds to another place

I will take you to where velvet lies, silky satin
Deeper still you turn me inside out
Locked together in this oasis
These whispered dreams to wake
Or to be my sweetest secret never told.

Diana Rae Harding

ANSWERS BY A MIRROR

As I stare in the mirror, what do I see?
A plain, blank face, staring back at me,
Deep in her eyes, I see torture and pain,
On the outside though, she's a bit vain!
Always trying to look her very best,
What will she wear tonight, her little black dress?
The pain you see has scarred her for life,
Cannot trust, always being deceived,
On the outside though she's bubbly and fun,
Wonder if tonight, she'll get another line spun!
Always there for family and friends,
The favours she's done, the list never ends,
She likes reading her stars
And has even taken up reading tarot cards,
They have helped her a bit,
Though she knows her life's incomplete,
People say she's quite attractive,
Size eight frame and so much to give,
Looking in the mirror and at that blank face
She asked her reflection,
Why give me more pain?
It's taken a lot to get through these past few years,
All she wants, is a normal family life,
Not the fools that give her trouble and strife,
As her only wish is to once again be a wife.

Angela C Taylor

THE SALAD OF THE BAD CAFÉ

Each afternoon I'd roam the streets,
Searching for some dingy hole
To rest my soles, my aching feet;
The greasier the better,
The wetter the weather
To suit my mood:
My rude, angry, desperate
Mood.

Food, she'd said, you'll need
Instead of those countless
Butts that rot your gut.
Nuts, yoghurt, fruit and salad -
Do take care - see you next week.

So I'd try to listen
And be very good,
Just as I'd tried
My entire childhood.

But the rebellion was
Winning, fighting, grinning
And as I lit a third cigarette,
I asked the waitress for a serviette
To go with my salad . . . chips and peas
And somewhere inside me
I felt rather pleased.

Pamela Bakker

BREAKING THE BARRIER

I cannot feel for you, my love,
Your pulsing joy or pain;
In pure intensity each moulds
Your growth, the path you gain.

Shut out, my powerless gaze is blurred
With tears unshed, unseen,
I strive to break the silent space,
Impenetrable, between.

You need not share your joy with me,
Its nurturing warmth feeds
Your world, completing trenchant dreams,
Sweet happiness and needs.

But what of pain that drips away
Deftly eroding peace?
Reach out to place the load on me,
Permit my guilt release.

What of my future? Gauge its worth
If you should leave my side.
Cold bleakness of eternity,
The gulf between too wide.

So test my feelings in your hands.
Can you now share my need
To draw alongside, whatever comes?
A mutual path indeed!

Eve Carter

UNDERSTAND ME

No one understands who I am,
The person I am inside,
Everyone seems so quick to judge me,
But I know I have nothing to hide.

Every little comment they make,
Hurts me like mad,
Every part of me crumbles,
In my heart I feel so sad.

If people could only see,
The care and love I have in me,
And all I have to give and share,
They'll know that judging me is not fair.

Making people see sense,
Is that hardest thing to do,
If they could open up their minds themselves,
They would feel the pain and hurt too.

No one understands who I am,
The person I am inside,
Everyone seems so quick to judge me,
But I know I have nothing to hide.

Debbie South

ALL OVER AGAIN!

The tears fall sadly,
I cannot see where I am to go from here,
How did I fail so badly?
It's just not plain to see,
The pressure's too much to take,
What is my mum going to say?

Proud of me whatever I achieve,
Why do I not see it that way?
Eventually it will come, the sense
Of failure will fade,
And I will be happy all over again.

Emma Jayne Barker

AN ORDINARY HOUSEWIFE

I am a woman, a mother, a wife
All of these things, dictate my life
But deep in my body where no one can see
There's a voice and it's saying
I want to be - *me*.

I want to be *me* - just for a day
Not to bother or care what people might say
I want to flirt or perhaps have a fling
And never to care what tomorrow may bring.

But I am a housewife, and I must obey
My conscience which speaks to me, everyday
It tells me to clean, to wash and to cook
At other men, I should never look.

But sometimes I tire of the work and the strain
And the pressures which build up in my brain
But just when I think, do just what you feel
To hell with the work and preparing their meal
The face in the mirror I realise is me - it's saying,
I'm helpless, *I love them you see.*

Angela Soper-Dyer

WHY?

Why do you accuse me
Of being too sentimental?
You fall in and out of love
Like Don Juan once did,
As long as the ball lands in your court
You are quite content.
Is it sentimentality that makes me care for you?
I think not - it is what one calls love.
I love you but you just put up with me
Or so you have told me repeatedly.
Why did you marry me?
Was it for convenience
Someone to cook for you and clean for you
Or was it someone to keep you company
When you came home after your latest conquest
My sentiments lie in what we once had
Not what we have now
Exciting new, fresh love once
Now gone stale on your part
I am a one man woman
I would not like to say what you have become
The seven year itch clawed you to ribbons long ago
Of course I am sentimental, I hoard my precious moments
Covet them like a once upon a time story
A fairy tale that never was true
Now the magic has all vanished
I stand defeated, once bitten twice shy
As I wish you a final goodbye.

Eleanor Dunn

WHO NEEDS A MAN?

An independent woman
I'm happy as I am
I've grown to be much stronger
And no longer need a man

I've assembled my own tool kit
Bought a manual for my car
With a neat new kitchen gadget
I can open any jar

I've plumbed in my own washer
Fixed a leak under the sink
And dealing with a blown fuse
Doesn't even make me blink

So why am I now sat here
A pathetic shaking jelly
Tears rolling down my face
And a churning in my belly

Where is that inner strength
That's developed here inside
Why have I lost my confidence
And want to run and hide

So much for independence
It almost makes me laugh
Destroyed by that great nemesis
A spider in the bath!

Annmarie

FREEDOM

You are trapped like a bird in a cage,
But I will open the door and set you free,
Fly away, don't be afraid to spread your wings,
I will help you,
I will fly with you up in the sky,
Above the clouds we will soar,
Feeling the warmth of the sun on our wings,
You're getting stronger and stronger now,
You are beginning to enjoy this freedom,
Soaring higher and higher,
I watch you flying away from me,
But I will be there to catch you if you fall,
I am your safety net
And the sun will set,
I won't forget,
Farewell my love,
Higher and higher you fly,
Now it's time to say goodbye,
Goodbye.

Angel Hart

NIGHTMARE

Silence, shattered by the slamming of a door.
Loud voices, shouting, frightening.
I pull the covers up over my ears, but,
the voices grow louder, angrier.
His, loud, and full of drunken rage.
Hers, soft and pleading, full of fear.
I cower deeper under the covers.

The sound of slaps, a scream.
Heavy footsteps coming up the stairs.
I go rigid, hardly daring to breathe.
Footsteps coming closer.
Please God. Let him go past.
Slowly I relax, my prayers are answered.
I am safe, at least for tonight.
Silence once more.

Jo Hannon

SPIRIT

I am a little acorn
Beaten by the breeze
Torn from my safe hold
Fallen to the ground
Spat on, trod on
Trounced into the earth
Buried and forgotten
In the mire and the dirt
But in the darkness I was safe
For I looked up to the sky
And slowly but surely
As I stood my ground
My roots took hold
And I grew with strength
No longer a little acorn
Beaten by the breeze
Now I am an oak
The strongest of all trees.

Wanda Round

WOODEN MARES

I came as Helen of Troy
My mind not in the claim
Legends are written up by men
And words don't weave the same.

I waited for the kings to come
To me in my white shift
My thoughts breeding free beneath
My body not my gift.

Feeling the irony
Balanced on the edge
The power my beauty held
With no true leverage.

I brought kingdoms down
Yet still I was purloined
No real say beyond
The stirring of their loins

None of them realised
The irony of the theme
We woke up too early
And you can't redream.

Women have stories, not history
No politics, premonition instead
Understanding of past feelings
Making future in my head.

A woman's knowledge
Is the biggest wooden horse of all
Sitting unasked within every citadel
Knowing when the walls will fall.

Jacquie Wyatt

A Woman For All Seasons

A woman friend is no respecter of time:
She'll sit by you in any season of your life.
Through winter when your heart is cold,
Your soul stripped bare,
Battered by howling winds of change.
She'll laugh and celebrate the spring with you,
And make you feel
Renewed, invigorated, full of hope.
She'll even bring a breath of spring
Into your poignant autumn days,
And make you search for gold
Amidst the dying leaves of your desires.
Then, ah, when summer comes!
Those times when all is well,
When threads of friendship
Weave a warm, embracing glow
Around you both,
Touching others' lives,
Breaking age-old isolations,
Reaching to those places
Where only women dare to go!
That's when you know
This bond is here to last.
What more could any woman ask?
True female friendship:
Life-affirming,
Courage-giving,
All-accepting,
Total trust.

Erica Wishart

Untitled

Each time you walked into the room, my heart skipped,
my stomach turned,
I awaited the sight of you at every moment.
A glance in the mirror, a flick of the hair,
Stand straight! Pull that stomach in! Dress well! Mind manners!
Eager to impress, I played the part of the perfect lady.
The need for your love no longer constantly troubles my mind,
No more am I an actress in a play called 'Lust',
The butterflies have flown, the beat of my heart has steadied.
I no longer strive to be all you could desire,
For I am myself, and am happy being me.

Sophie Lianne Perkins

Sexual Delight

The body out-laid
Thinking of flesh - a sensual appeal
All desire's mouth-watering delight
The lingering intent of lustful action - or
Great explosion of anticipation escaped
A fleshful presence
Of head and body and legs - nothing maintained
In dust made flesh - except the dark desire
Of carnivorous appetite.

Jennifer Cook

WHO AM I?

A daughter, a wife and mother,
Three roles, one like no other
A daughter to one I call Mum,
A wife to a husband to share a wonderful life,
A mother to our child aged just four,
Who I love, cherish and adore.

A person with many a different facade,
From time to time I reflect,
And hold myself in regard.

Me, a person in my own right, you see,
Sometimes, just me.

Dawn Fox

AFTER THE LOVE

After the love
I echo his smile
He wants to leave
We are like . . .
Strawberries without cream
A river bed without water
Sky without sun

After the love
I moved onto the dent in the sheets
You made on my bed.

Hattie Boulding

LET'S DO LUNCH

Talking strategy, business lunch chat
Discussing market share and estimated growth
Sexual undercurrents threaten milk pond.
Never touching physically but eyes telling all
Dive green depths to tidal waves of mutual desire
White table cloths become cotton sheets strewn across a bed
Knife cool to the touch like his back
Glass held too tightly, a hand clasped around a wrist
House red drank sedately dripped slowly over breasts
Ice cubes melted over hot limbs
Loganberries crushed against bare skin.
No apparent contact, but an afternoon of sex
No one aware of what passed between the professional pair.

K MacCormack

THE BIG 'C'
(A tribute to a wonderful woman)

C is for created, I am glad that you were
C is for caring, something you do to your detriment
C is for courage, which you have in abundance
C is for capable, which you have been to your cost
C is for constant, you are always there
C is for credit, something you rarely receive
C is for competence, at everything you do
C is for creative, in more ways that one
C is for *c*indness, if I may spell it like that
C is for cure, don't depend on it, just live
C is for cancer, a small part of you
don't get lost in it!

Gill Casey

TOSS POT

The game was on, it started slow, one player knew the rules
The stakes were high, the player played
He thought the others fools
He made the play and kept the scores and planned the route ahead
He took a shot, the risk paid off, he left the others dead

The moves were quick, the rules had changed, he bent them at his will
He saw the pot, he didn't think, he paused to take his fill
His moves were rash, he didn't care, the pot was all he saw
But rules are made for everyone, for every game a law

He tossed again, his shot was flawed, this player had to fail
His gamble cost him every gain (his card said go to jail)
His luck was out, he turned again to lock the stable latch
Then turned again to only find his chickens didn't hatch.

Angie Hennigan

RUTH

At last she's here, one longed for so much,
Tiny and fragile, so soft to the touch.
All the wondering and waiting for those long 40 weeks,
Now it's all baby lotion and talc on those chubby cheeks.
Perfect eyes and nose, ten fingers, ten toes,
How much she was wanted, God alone knows.
Now we've got her and at times it's tough,
But as parents, we have to take the smooth with the rough.
Though the burden at times weighs like a ton,
Everything is worthwhile when she whispers, 'I love you, Mum.'

W Rennison

The Heavens Wept

Grasping tight, her baby's blanket,
Screaming out, 'My son, my son.'
Her tight clasped hands were trembling
As she cried, 'What have I done.'
Her eyes approached the heavens
Fell on bended knees to pray
She pleaded, 'Father help me,
I gave my son away.'
She wept, and bowed her head in shame,
Overwhelmed with great despair,
Crying out, 'My Father, help me,
Please Father, feel my prayer.'
'My dearest child, lift up your head
And know that I am here,
I've heard your pleas, I've seen your pain
I've felt your every fear,
I have taken every journey,
Watched your face, your many trials
Carried you, when you were weary,
Come, take my hand, dear child.
I've placed stars high in the heavens
I've breathed life into the earth,
I've scaled mountains to their highest
To the trees, I gave them birth.
I've created raging oceans
Given life to deepest water
My precious child, the heavens wept
When I created *you*, my daughter.

Lift up your head, don't hide in shame
My precious, precious one
To you I give eternal love
To you, I gave away my son.'
She lifted up her tear filled eyes
Still crouched on bended knee.
'Thank you Father up in Heaven
For what you gave to me.'
This woman gave the greatest gift
The highest of a mother
She gave birth, she held her son
Then reached him to another.

Maggie Connolly

MOTHER

Awake at last and from the tortures of her sleep another day begins.
Alone to cope with four young lives,
their mouths to feed and fears allay.
They are in need, so work she must
at menial tasks for small reward, no questions asked.
Fair and falling hair sweeps round the face so pale,
but kindly eyes of brown alight as she sits by the gas firelight
and speaks of pennyworths of white, cold chips,
hot buttered pikelets almost burning her lips.
Sweet memories mist as eyelids close,
her family sleeps, now her repose.
Why did fate play such a quirk as this?
Are destinies devised in Heaven or self made,
and if self made, why suffer tortures of the mind,
physical pain and need.
To render her alone, who once was wife, friend and lover,
must life forever traverse this trial o'mother.

J Good

BULIMIA

I look into the mirror,
and what do I see?
A fat and ugly girl,
staring back at me.
My mother tells me I'm healthy,
my father tells me I'm slim,
I'm so obsessed with my weight,
when did this obsession begin?
I turn the pages of the glossy magazines,
Naomi and company dominate,
my soul becomes a bag of mixed emotions,
jealousy, admiration, desire and self-hate.
I seek refuge in my bathroom,
purging myself daily, of food I've eaten,
vanity and low self esteem have gotten the better of me,
my confidence is battered and I'm well and truly beaten.
My bones have become incredibly sharp,
I'm proud as they protrude through my skin,
my cheeks have become hollow and sunken,
but I'm happy at last because I'm thin.
The polka-dot dress that was tight some time ago,
fits me perfectly, like a glove,
my clothes flatter me now so much more,
I feel great now, I have so much self-love.
But I've become moody recently,
I fight with everyone around me from day to day,
I faint frequently and I'm emotionally suicidal,
I don't know how I can carry on living this way.
It's painful being a woman sometimes,
men have this perception of what you should be,
I feel like slashing my wrists at times,
then I'd be truly free.
Then one day, matters came to a head,
I'd collapsed and I was skeletal,
I couldn't move from my bed.

Suddenly I was rushed to hospital,
where they saved my life,
they diagnosed my condition as bulimia,
and stated that amongst young girls it's rife.
I'm a changed person now,
I eat for my health and to survive,
bulimia is dangerous and it kills,
I'm just so glad now that I'm alive.

F Buliciri

HONEY

Out of the eater, something to eat;
Out of the strong, something sweet.
Samson's riddle got them all going.
Anything for a new set of clothes.
Nobody would ever guess,
Honey from a lion's carcass.

That was why they had to cheat
And call upon his bride to prise the answer from him.
Feminine wiles, weeping and whining
Soon wore him down.

Ever the sucker for honey-lipped women,
Samson never learnt his lesson,
Fell into the same trap with Delilah,
Bringing about his own downfall.

Honey, sweet, natural, full of energy;
Good to eat, on toast or used in cooking.
But beware the honeyed lips of a *femme fatale*
Or, ladies, of a smooth-talking man.
For even the strength to kill a lion
Won't save you from the viper's fangs.

Kathy Rawstron

BLOOD TYPE

My bottom lip droops bleeding
my love is spilling out
The puddles are deep
and the stains are ripe
My heart lies savaged
overcome and numb
I cannot shout.
Your soft lies decayed my life
patiently drained me of fire.
Our once full love lies sleeping
our kisses hollowed out.
Your warm breath has turned stale
infected by your stench
destroyer of all desire.
You once flowed through me
now you ebb and churn consuming my veins, with melodic valour.
I stare back with cold eyes to our now feverish kisses
bleeding with anguish, till I'm clean of your type.
Flow,
sweet red poison.

Laura S Green

LOST IN TIME

Where am I going or where have I been
Maybe just hovering somewhere in between
Trying to move forward for there's no going back
Here in this vacuum I've lost the right track

All of my senses are out of control
With this affliction I can't even crawl
I'm locked in my world by a very strong key
Having a strange perception of everything I see

In reaching out with this passionate rhyme
Hoping you'll understand what I'm trying to mime
Wishing just once I could manage to join in
Wondering if I'm being punished for some long forgotten sin

Being at everyone's mercy is hard to accept
Feeling like a cast-off that someone had to reject
It would be easier, and I maybe wouldn't mind
If people understood and would always try to be kind.

Joyce Macdonald

PLAYING GAMES

We have been through so much,
but still, I cannot trust.
Wondering what you're saying
or the game you're playing.
Twisting the knife, but in whose back.
Oh what a crazy maze.

Manipulating people for your own ways,
but this is not just a simple phase.
Like cats fighting in the night,
squeals of pain or maybe your delight.

I have seen it all before,
only to ignore,
the vital signs and the clear cut lines.
You may live with your lies
but I will keep my pride
and sever all ties.
Goodbye.

Nicola Newton

WHEN I WAS LITTLE
(For my children and grandchildren with love)

When I was a girl, only five I'd be
Two sisters, a brother and little old me
Coming from school, looking forward to tea
What a fool I was thinking there would be something for me
When we got home, there's no one there
Again too often the house was bare.

Me mam's in bed, Dad's home from sea,
We always knew, my sister and me!
'Get out and play,' down the stairs he'd yell!
Kept in the street, till his belly was full.
Something for us, what a load of bull
Sent to bed in dirty clothes, pangs of hunger falling apart
Cold and hungry, he had no heart!
What we'd done nobody knows
But one thing's for sure, we'll be glad when he goes.

Next day at school, what a story I'd tell
So no one believed me, 'What the hell!
He'd hit us like hell, with belt across bum
But bruises well hidden, with help from Mum.

Due back at sea, with not a word said
But ended up in hospital, with a slab for a bed
A heart attack, no future for him
His time had come!
Being paid back for all he'd done.

Now being 50 and a mum at 20
My kids came home to a house never empty
Filled with love and food a plenty,
With a dad who works, but home every day to stay
A dad like mine, my god, no way!

So count your blessings
And hold them with love.
Or you could end up like me,
The one above!

Margaret Turrell

LOOKING BACK ON GIRL GUIDES

I can't rest
when I'm trying to do my best,
there's something drives me on
till all my energy's gone.
To do my duty to God.
Where is he now, I can't find a sod
of earth to cling to.
What I need is you,
but even you can't bring me
the peace I need inside,
the wish that I could hide
from myself.
To serve the queen.
Does she know where I've been
and the steps I've trod?
Can she understand the turmoil,
is she closer to God?
To keep the guide law.
There's nothing I want more
than to return to the days
when life was so clear,
when I so much wanted to be near
and nestled in, all warm and cosy,
believing that life was pink and rosy.

Julia Owen

IMPACT

Everyone here except her.
Minutes tick by
and still she's not here.
Then, when anticipation is high
and her nails are dry, she enters.

Every head turns to take her in
she's dressed for sin from head to toe.
Her 'almost' clothes, her shoes, her hair.

For a second she stands
best side forward.
The clatter of a pin drop
heard above the testosterone surge
circling the room like a Mexican wave.

This is the stuff of Trollop and Cooper
or movies about white mischief.
Hardly to be expected in a village
more used to sensible shoes
and frill necked Sloane blouses
worn under cardigans.

An exotic creature brave but foolish
displaying her finery here.
Her first party as the new vicar's wife.

She steps into the room
heads turn away, stories continue,
punchlines applauded
and juicy gossip sipped.

But she is not forgotten
the next day
at the village shop
the talk is all about *her*.

Rona Laycock

IS IT ME?

'You don't understand me,'
She shouts through her tears,
'Why don't you listen?
When I tell you my fears.
No one respects me,
Not even you,
I'm a person, a human being
And I'm certainly not you.'

She is sat in the corner,
Crunched up on a chair.
Hair flowing wildly,
It's hard not to stare.
I try to console her,
Though inside I am mad.
How to deal with this tantrum,
This one is so bad.

I pause for a moment, indecisive
I want to just leave her
To shout back, maybe cry.
But the mother takes over,
I know what to do,
Walking towards her,
She seems far away.
My hand touches her shoulder,
She falls into my arms,
'I'm sorry Mum,' she cries
'I don't mean to hurt you,
You just don't understand,
My life is so awful,
Were you ever twelve?'

Carolyn McCulloch

CITY 8AM

Never a smile, always a sneer,
Of all the people I steer clear.
Rushing and pushing through the street
I find myself under their feet
I'm in the way wherever I turn
My trampled feet of no concern.
To cross the road is a chore,
Step off the kerb and hear the roar

Of taxis and buses speeding past
Motorbikes with horns a blast.
Down the subway, follow the throng,
Skirt by the busker singing his song.
Up the steps, past the coffee place
Savour the aroma but keep up the pace.
Nearing the office with a sharp left turn
Cursing the need of the money I earn.
Climbing the steps to the revolving door.
Enter. And my working day begins once more.

Michelle Borrett

TWO SEASONS

We came in the summer,
Me and my own,
Alone,
Showed to our room,
Bed, basin, open window.

Fear made me leave,
Fear made me stay,
Granite in my heart,
No more of me,
To give to him.

A lot got easier,
Some things got worse,
Lessons learnt,
Good, bad,
All are valuable.

We leave in the rain,
We make a new start,
I had all this planned,
And we'll make it work out.

Lorna Ledger

JJ

My heart is pumping
A thousand times a minute
In anticipation for your first word
I watch your lips as they slowly open
Then without warning but with total individuality
You start to speak
At that moment of impact
I feel weightless
Unable to make contact with the ground
I fly away, float away
I met you when I was 20
But I feel like I've known you all my life
You're the vision I've kept locked deep inside
You are the one, the one I've been searching for
You can melt me with one word
Break me into a million pieces
And scatter me along the horizon
You are my world.

Sarah Moore

CUT OFF YOUR EARS

She learns rage inside.
Plan organised, her path crosses.
Stepping over the line.
Glorious pure spirit.
Shrapnel deliver the lamb.
Embedded beneath performance.
Feather bed dream-like essence.
Perfectionist uniquely wrapped.
Event imagined for a moment.
Chilled walk finished.
Malnourished society non-stop.
Attention seriously guaranteed.
Undeniably tasteful words.
Predictability sadly focused.
Taste all bad news personally.
Admit colossal rift.
Similar gentle parting.
Perfectly cornering storm.
Seek what you see.

Sharron Hollingsworth

FEAR...

... has a taste, a smell,
a pungency that all can tell

... has a look, a sound,
plain to all who are around.

... has a depth, a feel,
will none who loves me dare to steal?

My cup of fear, come now and share.
Ignore its stench, come if you dare.

Turn not your head from stricken eyes,
do not you hear my silent cries?

Take up this hand, foul as disease
and with its passing, give me ease.

Sue Bentley

TWISTED IMAGE

Excuse me, I said,
Just really, who are you?
Think you're something special?
Like Hell I think I do!
What right have you to think
You can do what you say you can -
You think you're not that stupid?
You know less than a man!
For men they are the great,
The self-opinionated race
They wallow in your grief
And fart derision in your face.

Excuse me, stupid woman
        Don't dare to look away . . .

Again her mirror spoke
(as it did so every day).

Trisha Porter

I Know How It Feels

What do you do when you've got no friends?
It seems that way as if your life ends.
You hear voices and wonder what they can be.
Your mind is vague and you seem all at sea.
You mumble a 'word salad' which does not make sense,
And rise to act hotly in your defence.
As you first sense the symptoms you are not sure,
What you're suffering. Could there be a cure?
The doctor says you should go into hospital for a rest.
You wonder what on earth is best.
And when you go in, it is at first
Of your own free will. Which is worst?
Then to go in by force? But soon,
You are under a section and it may be June
Of next year when you come out.
Time seems like eternity without a doubt.
You may be violent and rant and rave.
You do your best to get better and save
Your sanity and mind.
The nurses are sometimes kind.
You are on drugs and tablets and pills.
Electric treatment is scary and fills
You with apprehension. What on Earth
Made you feel this way? What were you like at birth?
The drugs have side effects and make you feel
As if you are on the edge of an abyss so real.
You have occupational therapy which is a help.
You knit and sew and paint you own self.
You think, 'Can this be happening to me?'
All you are and were and will be

Seem to melt in a daze. Of course it's the drug.
Largactil, Serenace, Kemadrin. What bug
Can cause this illness? Is it a germ?
That eats away at your mind like a worm?
And when you get better life seems to change.
It seems to take on a new perspective and will range
From your mind to your outlook.
People will read you like a book,
And say, 'Didn't I tell you, you would improve?'
In hospital you had visitors who would move
You with their kindness and cause you to cry.
They would say, 'You will get better by and by.'
And at last you are better but still on pills.
You might be on them for years and it kills
You to think there are still side-effects
That worry you and cause you to affect
An indifference to the future. But you think,
It will be a long time before you sink
Into another madness. At last
The worst is over and in the past.

Christine M Wilkinson

FOOD FOR THOUGHT

I am a lady pensioner who
Just can't make ends meet - oh what shall I do?
I remembered my dad grew veg through the war,
With an allotment we could have veg galore.
I'm busy ploughing through seed catalogues and book,
My husband calls out 'Gardening on TV, you really must look.'
On my birthday, presents arrive at the door,
Packets of seeds, compost and still there's more.
Gone are the days of high heels and perfumed smellies,
It's now insect repellent and a stout pair of wellies.

M Connelley

R

Sunshine day
Pulled in an alleyway
Pushed on a wall
No escape at all?
Hands all over
Too scared to breathe
Tight fitting skirt
Not easy to remove
Tights in the way
He'll make me pay
Out of his pocket
Shiny knife did I see
Thought this was the end for me
All of sudden
Inner strength did show
Get off you coward!
Then I kneed him a blow
He fell to the floor
And then he let go
I ran like the wind
Not waiting to see
If the man with the knife
Was coming for me
Into the light
Saw people at ease
Not knowing the pain
That had rained down on me.

Deborah Coltman

PALE PINK CARDIGAN

A pale pink cardigan flashes
In a spinning puddle,
As iron red spokes
Screech and grind to a halt.
Rings of thick, black rubber
Hover above mud
And cower beneath
Rust-ridden chains.
A slippy stairway of moss and wood
Climbs to Everest's peak
With a cold, clinical chrome descent
To a dirt pond on landing.
A Hansel and Gretel wake
Of crunching crisp bags and a
Clinking band of broken bottles
Leads through netting wire
At dusk;
Silence creeps into alley shadows,
The figure at the window retreats,
And darkness looms over
Fat, sweaty fingers
Plucking the sleeping pale pink cardigan -
It's going back to his house;
As playtime is done.

Cynthia Browne

ME MYSELF...

I'm a lesbian,
Not a alien from outer space!
I'm a lesbian,
Not a threat to the human race!
The government wants to condemn me as queer and perverted
But Elton John is welcome at Downing Street, as are all his taxes
In the treasury . . . hypocrites . . .
Clause 28 will be a noose round my neck if IDs get selected.
So life will get harder even if I try to lead it well.
My sexuality is not talked about in family circles
I feel I let my parents down being childless and a lesbian.
I did not choose my life, it was given to me free.
Along with these feelings I could not live a lie.
Marry some poor man and have children always wishing differently
All I want is a bit of equality and a bit of fairness
When I see couples holding hands I think, if that was me
I'd be laughed at, spat at or worse because I love my own sex
Here on earth.
So next time homosexual issues are raised just remember me,
I love animals and nature, try to help those less fortunate
And by the way, I'm gay!
I won't pervert your children or scare your cat
Or even steal your underwear off the washing line!
My sexuality is second nature to me, I don't flaunt it.
You may see me down your street as I don't have a brand mark
On my forehead reading 'Lesbian, keep away'.
The end of this epic is now in sight
A point perhaps I've made
For a little more compassion to all along life's way.

Liz Osmond

CAMEO

Deep-sea eyes skin sun-tinted,
5ft small and quick and active.
Dancing along with withered hip,
Trying to hide each faulty step.
Unaware my pretty mother
Of secret admiration.

Sensitive Bohemian lady,
Artistic, moody, kind and caring.
My mother welcomed every stranger,
Anywhere she'd talk and banter.
Scattered sunshine to the lonely,
Animals especially mattered.

Five other siblings shared her childhood,
Some days barefoot, some days with plenty.
Running wild, their schooling stinted,
Short-sighted eyes, frustrated learning,
Artist parents intent creating
A child in clay.

Through war and peace and changing lifestyles,
Through widowhood and ageing years,
My mother limped, living her story,
Memories shadowing a quiet face,
Unaware, my gentle mother
Of undying gratitude.

Eleanor Hamilton

FOOL'S GOLD

Little darlin', what song is in my heart tonight?
Little darlin', what pain eclipsed my mind tonight?
What shadows lurk unseen tonight?
Oh darlin', the grief won't us unite.
Have you become my one lost soul?
Am I devoid of conscience, bereft, a hole?
Unfulfilled by a spirit, set there to calm,
And not plugged up by 'love stuff balm'?
How should we progress our path?
Are we supposed to splice the half,
The third, the quart, that says we're us
The third, the quart, that they call lust?
What will really come of you and me?
Our frail existence, tumbling, never free,
Enclosed by guilt and pointless lies,
Forever held by loved ones' cries.
Time has passed now, since we parted,
Our lives struck chords and then departed
But on the platform standing bold
We saw our train run through with gold
Little darlin', that is where the sun went
Little darlin', that is what God sent.

Andrea Chapman

LIMBO

A sudden feeling of frustration,
That strange desire to cast off present state
And rise refreshed - another being.
Born anew! with destiny at my command,
Fate mine to arrange.
To go forward ever.
To cease the endless fleeing.

To grasp the morning in my hands.
To reach and touch the day.
To lie and feel the night.
To run and taste the wind.
To see the beauty that is life.
To be - and not to count the cost.
To leave the many - to join the few.

Valerie Spiers

CHOOSE

I choose to give up suffering
I choose to give up pain
I choose to give up struggle
And enjoy my life again.

I choose to give up poverty
I choose to give up lack
I choose now to be generous
Start giving something back.

I choose to give up arguing
I choose to give up strife
I choose to take the path
That least resists the rest of life.

I choose to give up loneliness
I choose, instead, to share;
I choose to love and be loved;
To be cared about, and care.

I choose to give up feeling hurt
I choose now to forgive;
I choose to let resentments die
So I can start to live.

Gayna Florence Perry

THE TRAMP

He sleeps on the park bench
His belongings in a bag
Asking passers by
'Have you got a fag?'

I wonder what catastrophe
Made him live this way,
And if I dare to ask him,
Would he really say?

You think him dumb and stupid
But that's not really the fact
He is very clever and polite
Conversation full of tact.

He spends his time just thinking
Of how the world should be
And as he talks of peace and calm
His face lights up with glee.

It is a demonstration
Albeit on his own
No one takes any notice
If you sit and moan.

So next time you pass by a bench,
Don't judge too hastily,
He has a home, he has a mum,
You've guessed, that's right, it's *me*.

Angela Severn

NOT EVEN LOVE

I don't have to tell you everything
Do you think I owe it to you?
When you don't even listen
And behave like you do.

When we were married
Such a long time ago
I thought I could love you forever
Now your grey, thinning hair
An outlook of 'I couldn't care'
Means that I have nothing to share
Not even love.

We have both slowly gone
Our own separate ways
Different types of enjoyment
Fill our separate days.

We have the children
A blessing I suppose
But the dislike towards you
Is something that grows.

Perhaps I'm as bad
Perhaps I've not been that good
Perhaps I'm just sad that I
Didn't stay single - I most definitely should.

Wendy George

GATHER ROUND, MY SISTERS

Now gather round my sisters, and let us all discuss,
Ways and means to change the world, and make a bloody fuss!
I think we should have compassion, and we should spread it wide,
So if you are a careless sort, then take leave of my side.
We'll let no petty bitching divide this merry band,
We'll pray the powers of the Earth to join us hand in hand.
We'll take this land and make her well with our hearts, our souls, our heads,
And the skills employed in all our roles will stand us in good stead.
And soon we'll see hands reaching out, across the continents,
And we will not be governed by pounds, euros, dollars, cents.
We will not tolerate being told what it is we need,
We will not tolerate suffering for vanity, 'cleanliness' or greed.
We'll learn to take the time to see the beauty in this world,
And hope will spread from town to town where our flag is unfurled.
We'll take care of the children who have no love to share,
And show the world that we can help, we *can*, we *will* be there.
Let's educate our children so hope lasts when we're gone,
We'll show the world a woman's worth - yes, even with our clothes *on!*
So come on every woman and take and make your part,
I know you have it in you, I know that you are smart.

So gather round my sisters, and let us all discuss,
And in the meantime - seize every opportunity to go out and make a fuss!

Jo Stott

WHAT ABOUT ME?

I live in this world
but no one can see me.
My world is my bedroom
but no one can hear me.
Too exhausted to move
won't someone believe me?

So much pain
how can I stand it?
Isolated and alone
how can I handle it?
Can't someone help me,
do I deserve it?

Ruth Cottis

TIME OF LIFE

It must be my age, I hear myself say,
I forget things easily, go hot, in an odd kind of way,
It must be the change, I think that's what they call it,
Most men don't understand, not one little bit.

I can fold up in tears, at the drop of a hat,
I'm 48, so that must be that,
Mood swings are there, some good, some bad,
No one asks what makes me so sad.

The doc says that's probably what it will be,
How long does this last, is what's bothering me.
Some days I feel 90, some days 23,
I must see the doc, for some of that stuff, HRT.

A woman is fragile, a woman is tough,
But there comes a point where she's just had enough.
The things that we go through, from cradle to grave,
Some sail right on through there, some have to be brave.

If I return to this Earth,
I don't want to give birth,
Or do mid-life crisis and family plan!
I just want to come back and return as a man.

Janet Swindlehurst

DOT'S OLD SHED

My husband's pulling down our shed he built so long ago,
The reason why he built it, well only he would know.
'You cannot knock a nail in,' as I would often say,
My husband said, 'I'll show you' and proceeds to knock away.
With no proper wood available, he decides to use some scrap,
Puts on a pair of overalls, gets his tool box and his cap.
He started with this old leg from a bed,
The seat from a chair,
A cupboard door that was red.
He hammered and sawed, this shed he would master,
'I'm bleeding,' he cried, 'you'll have to get me a plaster.'
When he was finished he stepped back with pride,
But I saw my neighbour coming and decided to hide.
I saw him look as he came by, he'd never seen the like,
He lost his concentration and fell right off his bike.
It's been a constant source of amusement
And I see it every day,
For as the wind begins to blow,
The shed begins to sway.
But at long last it's coming down, for him it's quite a wrench,
But he's informed me to my horror, that he's going to make bench.

Beverley Rees

DISAPPOINTMENT

Catacomb around you, waiting for your change,
You should grow and develop and then it won't feel so strange.
I can hear you breathing, it's running all over my skin,
Weaving around my body and touching me deep within.

Slowly you begin hatching, as if just given air,
You begin to shake and shiver and all I can do is stare.
Gradually you awaken and echo a loud yawn,
I'm now sitting lonely as if just one of your million spawn.

Am I just another, just all the same as the rest?
Is that why you don't cover me when I lay and rest?
Or am I someone special, like in one of your dreams,
If so, why don't I feel it, it's not the way I thought it would seem.

May-Tyra Tirén

WEIGHING UP THE SEASONS

Each season is magnificent with nature 'the mainstay'
Like drawing up a balance sheet - we find 'credits' outweigh
The 'debits' that do appear somewhere from time to time
But many wondrous gifts so free - makes us feel sublime.

Spring appears breathtakingly, a lovely lingering scene
As buds burst forth with trees so tall and leaves of brightest green
Primrose, violet and daffodil, what happiness they bring
Along with catkins, new-born lambs and the bird upon the wing.

Summer brings the sunshine and crowds flock to the sea
The butterfly delights us all as he joins the busy bee
Cornfields a blaze of yellow, dotted with poppies red
Such a joy to savour, as we make our way to bed.

Autumn leaves that rustle in many shades of brown
Chestnuts and conkers thickly displayed and patterned on the ground
Are firm favourites with the young - their eyes sheer gleaming bright
Gathering up their splendid Guy to burn on Guy Fawkes night.

Winter creeps upon us, unfortunately too soon
Gazing at night across the sky to a shiny moon
With snow so white, a robin sings - what a little dear
Proclaiming with his merry song, 'Spring will soon be here.'

Betty M Bennett

BLUE DAYS

Your silhouette painted black upon the wall,
Dancing with the shadows,
You've danced with them all.
Perhaps you have forgotten,
In your wayward crawl,
Searching for a horizon,
In the aftermath of a fall.

For your blue days are nearly over now,
Reminiscent lessons of tear-stained nights,
A mass of confusion and traumatic fights.
There was a child that became a woman,
And a woman that retained the child.
The cold winds are changing,
Calmer now, almost mild.

These are the blue days,
A time of recuperation from heavy sedation,
Of welcomed hope and isolation.
Fluid time to heal all wounds,
And learn from past mistakes,
To cleanse softly all the seeping cracks,
And mend up all the breaks.
To forgive but not forget,
Yet to trust without regret.

A silent recovery,
From this passing phase,
Be humble now,
In this tangled maze,
For these must surely be the blue days.

Luthien Lark

THE ROOM

I stand alone
in the empty stillness
remembering

Pretty pink, girlie frills
soft toys around a single bed
the cuddles and hugs
cries for 'Mummy' -
Comfort
Black clothes strewn
no visible floor
magazines, discarded letters, tapes
loud noise called music
dark curtains drawn against the world
door closed against us -
Anger
Books lying everywhere
papers from work
suits and jackets, smart skirts
a kettle, mugs, coffee
'Come in, let's talk'
thoughtful discussion, debate -
Advice
Packing, sorted chaos
then at last, quiet
only the boxes
cardboard boxes full of memories:
a daughter now a friend -
Love

Phyllis Yeoman

WINTER

Ears, hands and feet become huge lumps of nothing on a cold wintry morning
Grey clouds shadow the purpose of my life
The red rose, the yellow bell, all splashes of colour
Suppressed, oppressed and destroyed by the chill northerly wind
Blowing hard, determined, causing tree branches to flounce around like a sulking child
No escape from it possible
It sneaks up my skirt, down my chest
The most lecherous man alive could not be so effective - or so fast
People everywhere
Huddled in grey coats, black hats. An air of mourning reigns
For the sleeping beauty of an almost forgotten summer
Where can I find a prince to rouse her with a fiery kiss?

Chaoxter Reeves

THE SIBLING

My father that I never knew, you never knew of me.
I never saw your picture, I never felt your touch,
you did not know I walked this Earth and needed you so much.
I have a sister somewhere, and this I am certain of,
she is a lucky lady having you to love.
I prayed one day I would find you, but then - what would I do?
'Hello Dad, I'm your little girl.' Your reply, 'I don't know you.'

The years have passed, I sometimes cry,
I have now learnt you are in God's sky.
I miss you, Dad, I love you too,
I can never forget the dad I never knew.

Jill Foster

BODY HEAT

You demand
An inner warmth from me.

A woman fully charged,
Ironing your shirts,
I fold them neatly,
Tuck them into drawers.

But by night
The house glows darkly.
Sparking cells encircle
Switched on spots of light.

Later still, I heat your bed,
My central core wound tightly
Round your being,
My inmost flames maintain.

Valerie Hockaday

INNER VOICE

As days drift
through pleasure and pain,
turmoil and peace,
A muffled voice persists,
squeezed and squashed,
pushed and shunted.
With monotones
like a heartbeat
ever present.
Sometimes I hear it,
cautiously I listen
to the secrets within.

Kate Cowan

HOMELESS

There's nowhere to sleep, out in the cold,
A small cardboard box, the only comfort that I call home.
The shelters are full, full to the brim,
Only the concrete ice blocks in front of doors
- closed -
are left for me.
My companion by my side looks up, he whimpers.
His scrawny physique and scruffy white coat, now black
remains my only friend.
People walk by smiling, pretending they care.
No one offers help, no one believes me,
'You're a fraud,' they'd shout.
'Get a job,' they'd say.
'Haven't got a home, can't get a job,
Haven't got a job, can't get a home,'
the old cliché I'd cry.
Food is a fantasy, a luxury I can't afford,
Scraps from bins, the tiny amount of cash
- found -
supplies the only nourishment.
Now, sitting out in the streets was not the plan,
I won't wish this on any poor soul.
To watch the ignorance
of every man, woman and child.
All I long for is a warm, cosy bed
with food galore,
a bath to clean away all the hate
and grime of years gone by.
All I ask for is a little love and respect.
Is that too much to give?

Amy Zeglicki

HOW GOOD IT WOULD BE IF YOU WERE STILL HERE

I remember you so clear.
You were so much fun.
You were always happy.
You were my number one.
You always tickled me
And told lots of jokes.
Everybody loved you.
I remember you so clear.
You worked so hard
To get so far.
You always said to
Reach for the stars.
You spoke words of wisdom
That still stay with me today.
You give my confidence
And optimism in every way.
Thinking of you makes me strong,
It makes it all clear on
Why I want to go on . . .
I want to reach for the stars
For both me and you.
My memories of you are so good.
My memories of you are so clear.
They will always stay in my mind
And close to my heart so dear.
Every time I think of you
In my eye there is a tear.
How good it would be if you were still here.

Cathy A Gormley-Belle

FOUND OUT

Got up
Set light to your cheque books,
Watched them burn.

Put white shirts in wash with yellow dusters
And credit cards.
Watched it all go round at 90 degrees.

Ground up a chilli, rubbed in all your underpants,
Put them neatly back in drawers.

Put cat in cattery and dog in kennels.
Booked myself a month's holiday,
... you just got paid.
Put your passport in food disposal unit.

Reported all cards stolen
And changed account numbers.
Took car.

Did not leave a note ...
Hope she was worth it!

Moira Jean Clelland

WINDOW SHOPPING

As she sat looking at me
Her face set me thinking
I realised she was sitting there
Without even blinking

Her face was a palish white
And her hair was black
I thought that if she moved her head
Her face would crack

Her legs were slim and crossed
Her hands were on her tummy
I came to life and looked again
You guessed! She was a dummy!

Jill Fletcher

ACCEPTANCE

So much hurt, so much pain
why do I feel my crying is in vain?
The one that I want, the one that I need
is the only one that pays me no heed.

He says he loves me, he says he cares.
When I'm ill or I cry, he's just not there.
Bright and bubbly, happy as a lark,
then he'll be there, but not when I'm dark.

Ill and needy, black and grey
that's when he always runs away.
He cannot change, he never will
he doesn't understand what it's like to be ill.

I want to be bubbly, I want to be bright
but we all have days when we can't see the light.
I love to live, I love to laugh
so I'll forget him for now and go take a bath.

Sometimes I hurt, sometimes I cry
I'll accept him for him then there'll be no goodbye.
We took our vows, said we'd stay together
so there we shall be, always and forever.

Dawn Elaine Corner

Solitude

For 29 years we struggled along
Brought up our children and when they had flown,
He left me - for someone with youth on her side.
I was bereft, I'd lost all my pride.
For almost a year, I wallowed in grief
Cried for this man, who was no more than a thief,
Who had taken my best years, then cast me away,
Well, I finally came to my senses one day.
Life is too precious, I've wasted a year,
I'll look for a job, build a career.
I went into business and I didn't stop,
But fought like a Trojan, to get to the top.
He came back to see me, 'I'm sorry,' he said,
'can you ever forgive me, can I share your bed?'
'I'm sorry,' I said, 'but you had your chance,
she paid the piper, you wanted to dance.'
'Go back to your new wife, kiss and make up.
Go back to the children, whose lives you disrupt.
Go back and with them, build a new life,
Then just forget I was ever your wife.'
I visit my grandchildren, once in a while,
I wipe away childish tears, cherish each smile.
The parting brings sadness, but as I board the train,
I'm counting the weeks, until I see them again.
Life is tranquillity, living alone,
I answer to no one, my time is my own.
If at times I feel lonely, that's a small price to pay,
For the joy and contentment I find in each day.

Florence M Vass

First Kiss

I could see from the window
the shop where we were to have met
I ran down the stairs
not wanting to miss you.
I had only met you once, but I knew
I waited, lunchtime over
I walked, empty, back to work
thinking you hadn't wanted to see me
Later, I called you
we laughed about lunchtime
how we had missed each other.
An arrangement made for Saturday
again we laughed
was it the left lion as you faced them
or with your back to them?
We didn't want to miss each other again.
You were there waiting for me
I ran from the bus, not wanting you to leave
thinking I wouldn't be there
We spent the day laughing, joking
we had so much in common
Soon the town was empty
as we stood in the Market Square
You turned to me
and with all your courage, asked for a kiss.
I turned to you
and with all my body, gave you a kiss.
A kiss which has been etched into our lives
A kiss we will never forget.

Sheena Zeglicki

MANCHESTER TO CORNWALL

I enjoy camping under the stars
and spending cold evenings in clubhouse bars.
The reason we started was cos it was cheap
but then we discovered that we liked it a heap.

My children and I camp as much as we can,
the roof-box makes the car as tall as a van.
We pack it with all of the things that we need,
games and puzzles and stories to read.

We take with us all of the practical things . . .
like the cooker, the saucepans and lanterns on strings.
It's as if the car boot is made out of lycra,
it's amazing how much you can fit in a Micra.

We have travelled round and tried different sites,
staying at most of them two or three nights.
We've tried the Lake District, Wales and the rest,
but Cornwall is the place that we like the best.

We like it best sunny, but don't mind the rain,
we come back to visit again and again.
I used to come here when I was quite small,
with my mum and my dad and our dog and a ball.

I've been coming here years and the fun never ends,
I'm down here so often, I've made quite a few friends.
People say, 'Why Cornwall again? Try somewhere new!'
My answer to that is, 'Well, why don't you?'

Cornwall is great and my love for it has grown,
it's a place I would soon hope to be calling my 'home'!

Jane Colwell

ONLY A WOMAN KNOWS

Only a woman knows the moment of conception
That the start of a new life is not just a perception.
Only a woman feels that moment, when the scan
Reveals the result of her union with her man.
The feelings of happiness tinged with fear,
Lest things are not what they appear.
Only a mother knows the depth of grief,
If she miscarries this pregnancy - however brief.

Only a woman feels that first movement - that kick,
Was it wind? No, it was real. Oh dear! I feel sick.
As her body changes shape as the baby grows
How does this feel? Only a woman knows.
Then there is that moment of the birth,
Surely, the most exhilarating on Earth?

Feelings of contentment with baby at the breast,
A hint of exhaustion with little time to rest.
Feeling tearful and confused is called baby blues,
Is this what I want? Is there an option to choose?
They say it's hormones and that they will settle down,
That soon I will be out for a night on the town.

Only a woman knows the depth of this struggle,
With motherhood, career and home life to juggle.
So remember, as we traverse the road of life,
Balancing roles and dealing with strife.
It doesn't matter what wild oats a man sows,
The experience of childbirth - only a woman knows.

Jane Winney

ANNIVERSARY
(For Ed)

Look at this room -
Not very tidy!
But pretty enough
with lamps and flowers and
pictures and stuff.
And all the books - there were
never enough -
music too . . .

I look at this room without you . . .
Yet here you are in the
flowers you grew,
every spring coming through.
And all the things we
collected together
in time that would last forever.
And I still hear you say
'Not sure about that!'
but I usually got my own way.
And here you are in the music
we shared - the Chopin you
played on piano.
Clever old you!

In remembering these things
and the peace that it brings
here on my own
in whatever I do
always and ever, there's you.

Jo Lee

LIFELINE FROM MOTHER SHIP

Eager the mother
Pointing the way
Confident that observation
Is clear.
From distant light-years
She has a distorted view
Of present space.

She covers
She protects
from the explosion.
They are precious
Hard casing they have built
Out of necessity
To withstand
Nuclear blast.

Questioning
The corrosive brainwashing
That each instinctively
Knows to ignore.
Communication is vital
Barriers are down
In quiet moments
Triumphant
She is on target.

This only happens
When the moon is blue.

June Drysdale

THE LOVERS

Rip me apart and watch me bleed, see the flower alive before you,
Here the pod to fold your seed, there the joy you trod beneath you,
Push your fingers in the wetness, take no notice of my tears,
Blind the iris with your kisses,
Never let it see your fears.

Come - disembowel my fire with silence,
Pull the petals from my mouth,
Ignore the hand that moves to hold you,
The dream that freezes on the path.
Caress my skin and feel its pulsing, golden layers fly and fall,
Watch me - touch me - see me dancing,
Waiting for the night bird's call.

Come - be kind,
Honour me with death.
Say you loved me once,
Before you rest.

Susan Harwood

STRATEGY MEETING

Huddled in this airless space
I wonder why I agreed to come?
Testosterone oozes through the room,
An attempt to suppress me . . ?
I am whole; a professional like you
Why make me feel like a minx?
Silly innuendo shows your depth -
Surface cracks now visible.
Hello? Shut-up! Ask me a question!
You reach for the coffee and touch my arm.

Sharon Leaver

SOLITUDE

Calm is the moment
Caution is the stay
Macroscopic is the motion
Microscopic is the play
Biographic is the way
Grangerize the context
Tolerate the molestation
Veto the harum scarum
Enchain the mantling
Conversably mane the mammato
Manuscript the document
Vouch for the mannerly
Tell the chic madam to contribute
E M Purple the end
The documentary is now complete.

Sarah Margaret Munro

MUM'S HANDS

How suddenly it happens, before you realise
Your mother's hands before you,
But no, the hands are mine.
But time has repeated, quite an identical pair.
Mine are lined and dry now,
One could hardly compare.
The trials and toil she left behind her
Are now identical with mine,
So it goes on, continuing a series of our times.

Joyce Maud Carter

THE DANCE OF LIFE

I ran so fast that I almost fell over
Made all my choices, saw clearly the way
The dance that is life with her dainty hand beckoned
Her colours so vibrant, unable to fade.

Of silver and gold were the rings on her fingers
The softest of leather let feet celebrate
With the rise and the fall of the breath in her body
The drape of the fabric a madrigal played.

In mystical spirals her hair polkaed waistward
Revealing, concealing a hand that would ache
To hold in her palm all the fruits of the harvest
To sing all the notes of the song that she made.

Yet greatest of all was the truth in her eyes
Fulfilment of every dream's efforts to pray
Defiant of word, separated from body
I watch, I wait, I participate.

Gaynor Dawn Coleman

HOW LUCKY I AM!
(Written for Mum in a nursing home)

How lucky I am
To have landed here
Found new friends
And lost my fear - of being alone.

How lucky I am
To have those who care
See to my needs
Always there - attending.

How lucky I am
When darkness falls
Someone's there
To hear my calls - for help.

Sandra Kinnear

RESTLESS

As we lie I watch you from behind
So that you cannot see me
(I think of how you change
From one day to the next
Yet somehow always stay the same)

Take this breath like it might be my last
One last irrational thought before morning
Back off before you notice,
I know you don't like me so close as this
Reckless

I shouldn't think like this
But to turn your back makes me all the more restless
Where do I put my hand? Do I search for yours?
Keep it to myself
Turn my back to face yours

Keep you at length
And pretend to have a say
My stupid preoccupations I'm afraid to let you see
But
In the dark with love as I am, I am dying for you to hold me

Helen Looker

YOU ARE WHAT...

The dreaded question
And you, what do you do?
The eyes display
If not real interest
At least some kind of curiosity
Me?
Prefabricated answer
Blushing with defensiveness
Digging up the past to
Show I once was someone
That justifies an interest in
Me
The facts of my existence
Make them turn away
I stay at home
I am a mum
Wait, there is more to
Me.

Regine Seely

LOVE OF LIFE

To be a woman is very lucky,
Having a baby and feeling clucky,
The world seems to have a glow,
There is no time to feel low.

First love makes us feel
As though the world's our oyster,
The rosy glow seems quite real,
Until we are made to loiter.

'You'll regret it,' I hear them say,
But who wants to listen,
We carry on come what may,
The whole world seems to glisten.

I look back, not in anger,
Enjoyment was the order,
A war did not even stop the clanger,
Regrets we could not afford-er.

Sylvia Ash

BIRTHDAY

'How do you feel?'
'Oh warm inside.'
'It tore my heart when she just cried.'

'This is your child.'
'Then give her to me.'
With eyes full of wonder what do I see?

Tiny pink ears, the colour of shells,
I close my eyes and see bluebells.
Sweet smelling grass, washed with dew,
This is my heart, I give it to you.

Skin so soft, satiny silk,
I kiss her cheek, she tastes of milk.
Biting my lip, she matters so much,
With uncertain wonder, I just want to touch.

When she smiles, it warms my skin,
When she cries, the sun goes in.
I drown in eyes, blue and new,
This is my life, it belongs to you.

Irene Smith

SNAPSHOT

Sitting on a bench together. Smiling for the camera,
His arm around me. You'd think we were happy!
But our legs are crossed away from each other.
I'm turning away from him, but leaning on him.
Not that I can for real.

Funny how the picture shows me
Relying on *his* strength. In reality it's the other way round.
I have to actually fall apart in front of him
Before he will take up the struggle for me.
Shame really. It means that for most of the time
I don't need him.

So what am I saying here? That I don't need him?
I don't need his refusal to take any responsibility or think for himself.
I don't need the complete lack of any need to tidy as he goes,
To clear up a spill or think ahead in order to make life easier.
Is he aware of the chaos he causes? I doubt it.

When we're together on holiday, things are great!
But that's after I've made all the decisions,
Organised the packing and the travelling,
Secured the house and cancelled the milk.
If only he would help me out occasionally, take some of the
Strain of living,
Be a partner instead of another responsibility.

If I changed words for actions I'd spoil what we have. So I keep quiet.
It helps me having me to talk to. Helps get things into perspective.
A tidy house isn't everything. We don't fall out about important things
Like trust and respect. He doesn't drink too much or spend too much
And as far as I know he's never been unfaithful.

I have three children, not two. Sometimes he calls me Mum,
Then corrects himself quickly. Well maybe that's what he needs.

Maybe that's what I need him to need.

Jose Kent

TIAMO SEMPRE

I board a bus of broken hearts, the ticket is one way.
Just take a seat, press repeat and watch life slip away.
You always say, 'Could have done better.'
You always say, 'Wish I had.'
But if life had been kinder, if it hadn't been so bad,
Would we have learnt our lessons that fate left for us,
Or still be sitting, with regret, and lonely on this bus?
My days now are long and empty, the nights are worse still,
Sitting dazed in front of the telly is making me feel ill.
What can I do to change it? I haven't got a clue,
I might as well embrace it, I'm dying without you.
Those things I thought important, the things that made me care,
The things that excited me are nothing without you there.
I'm losing my grip, I've lost all touch,
I hate this world, cos I loved you so much.
I hate the weather, I hate the outside,
I hate my life and the tears that I've cried.
I hate being bothered to get up each day,
I hate doing anything, you're so far away.
Pain racks my soul for the touch of your hand,
My heart I shattered, like a million grains of sand.
I wish I could switch off, like the snapping of a light,
Not feel anything for you, not today, tomorrow or tonight.
But to do that you'd have to rip out my heart
And hold my nose to suffocate, till me and life depart.
I love you Maurizio, I honestly do
And if things were different, I'd be with you.

Carla Lobina

THOUGHTS OF A MUM

The wind howls, rain beats on the windowpane,
It is night again.
The cat purrs by the hearth, the fire all aglow,
Home is cosy and warm.
The children all asleep, snuggled down in covers soft,
Rosy cheeks and tousled hair.
Tomorrow is another day.
In the morn, voices will wake me from my slumber,
Children dressing, never quiet.
All is bustle, all is hustle. School time is here,
The bus awaits.
Hats, coats, satchels, shoes, last minute rush,
Then peaceful quiet descends - hush.
After a few hours my chores are done.
'Mum doesn't go to work. She stays at home.' What fun!
One day the satisfaction will be theirs.
Healthy children with no cares,
A cosy home, food to eat,
Love and happiness theirs to keep.

Iris M Burgess

END OF AN ERA

The only way now is up, they say,
We will live to fight another day,
Our hearts may be heavy, our eyes may cry,
When at last comes the time to say goodbye.

The future for us, for now is unknown,
But one consolation, we don't stand alone.
We've worked very well and hard (so we thought)
It seems just a pity it's all come to nought.

But with heads held high and backs that are straight,
We won't look back as we go through the gate.
We have to look forward and go in with pride
Then no one can say, 'Well, they never tried.'

Maureen Leveridge

MELTING MOMENTS

Melting my heart,
Melting my mind,
Treat so tasty,
Treat so kind.
Opening the box with lavish trim
Choosing a *chocolate* from within.
I place into my mouth to taste
Chocolate heaven, with a grin!
It melts away
Like instant whip.
More *chocolate*
At fingertip!
Chocolate of dark brown or light,
Chocolate, chocolate, sheer delight!
Such pleasure from within a box,
Resisting them with all my might,
I have to eat
Another one,
I am having
A lot of fun.
The last *chocolate* is there to eat,
I weaken and show my defeat
And pick it up, placing in mouth,
I make it last and feel complete!
Oh chocolate!

Linda Knight

REMEMBERING NAN

I thought of you the other day
And it brought a smile to my face -
Sitting on a rock by the riverside,
Which was always our special place.

It was your birthday and I had promised you
That I would remember you every year
And even though time passes by so quickly,
I still managed to shed a tear.

These days I know you are guiding me
In my dreams and throughout the day,
I know you're with me, protecting me,
In your own very comforting way.

I walked through a garden yesterday
With a friend who knew you well,
She listened to me as I talked of you
And the thoughts I wanted to tell.

We chanced upon a wooden chair
With a carving which caught my eyes -
It was half a sun, behind a hill,
With rays that reached to the skies.

I couldn't decide if it was rising or setting;
And said to my friend, so very wise,
'As long as our dreams outweigh our memories,
The sun will always rise.'

Kim Thomas

DECIDED

You know, I've decided,
If there's another life to live
After we shed this mortal coil,
Such as it is,
If there is, I'm telling you now
When I come back,
Sometime, some how,
won't be a bird or a plant or a cow!
I'll be a man!
Oh yes! A man.
How easy can you get?
9 to 5 and feet put up,
Food on table, name on cup.
(Been at work all day -
Keeping a roof over your head.)
Looked after all their life,
first their mother, then their wife!

When does a woman's work get done?
Men, at some point they retire!
Women, we go on till we expire!

So no, when I come back,
I'm taking it easy, having some fun!
Is 'my' dinner cooked? The ironing done?
Oh yeah, please God, send me back if you can,
But please, yes please, make me a *man!*

Rose Childs

WITH YOU

With every kiss you stole some of my breath,
With your touch you exposed my body,
With whispered 'I love yous' you drowned my mind,
With the touch of your hands you took my warmth,
With your laugh you caught the ends of my smile,
With your dance rubbed off the swing in my walk,
With your head on my pillow you shattered my dreams,
With you gone, you took the sweetest thing I've ever known,
With your promises you stole my future,
With that tone of voice you killed my trust,
With your betrayal you darkened my eyes,
With your indifference you leave me lonely,
Where your heart beat right next to mine,
my rhythm followed to leave an echo,
Take care because you're holding a piece of my soul.

Amber Jane Fossey

PLATITUDES

I've cooked your favourite dinner
Thank you darling - I love you
I've washed that shirt and socks you wanted
Thank you darling - I love you
I've sewn that button back on your blue shirt
Thank you darling - I love you
I've left you a sandwich in case I'm late back
Thank you darling - I love you
I must do the shopping today
Yes darling I will drop you off - you could walk back -
It will save me trying to park - er -
You haven't got much to get, have you?

Dee Wilson

MERLOT FOG

The petit pois and the plaice were to blame,
as we writhed around without shame,
as the 60s music blared out loud
and the Merlot wine formed a comforting cloud
of confusion, fogginess and lust
as I danced behind my voluptuous bust
that was dripping milk for my three month child
while her poor mother was going wild
with desire for Billy, so seductive and cool
I danced naked like a total fool.
I shed my role as wife, cook and mother,
like a chameleon I became a lover.
When all my passion was spent and done
I rolled over and fed my hungry one.

Ruth Belton

MESSAGE OF LOVE

My dears, I'm saying these words so true
Your children are only lent to you.
I laid down guidelines in early years,
Put up with naughtiness, tantrums and tears.
Before I could blink the time had passed
You were married, grown up at last.
You'll find your children are just like you
Love them and help them whatever they do.
Don't break your heart if they don't stay near
They won't go far, you've nothing to fear.
For your children, when you let them go,
You have forever - don't you know?
The guidelines you laid, as I did for you
Will never waver, but carry them through.

Patricia M Whitehead

THE DAYDREAM

She wakes with the dawn and pulls on her gown.
It's time for the breakfast, she'll have to go down
Into the kitchen and put on the eggs.
First though, the bathroom - the shower and loo
Today is so special, it's a job interview.
She must wash her hair and hot-wax her legs.

The kids are awake and waiting for help;
The dog needs his walk - he lets out a yelp.
She'll never be ready and looking her best.
It's a typical day - the mother comes last.
Start dressing the kids, get their breakfast.
When that's all finished, she'll then get dressed.

The kids are now fighting and throwing their food.
This day's a disaster, it just is no good
To even attempt for a life of her own.
Her husband comes downstairs and into the room
He's late for his meeting and he starts to fume,
'Where's my clean shirt? This is like a battle zone!'

The breakfast is over, the pots are all dried
The family are ready, they all go outside.
The car leaves the drive - she's alone now, at last.
She makes a black coffee and sits in the chair
Now to get ready and fix up her hair.
But look at the time! She must do it fast!

She's ready; she stops; she looks in the glass
As she walks to the door, through which she must pass
She sees her reflection; her hair neat and curled.
It just isn't possible, she can't get a job.
It was just a daydream, she thinks with a sob.
She's needed at home - this is this woman's world.

Anthea Bramley

WOMEN'S PROGRESS

When I was young my one aim in life
Was to find a good husband and be a good wife
To raise a family in the traditional way
Cooking and cleaning for most of the day

But we were quite happy with our lot
Immense satisfaction was what we got
Happy children, contented spouse
Home baking, sewing, tidy house

But things are changing and opening new doors
There's more to life than polishing floors
We're a new breed of women, us working wives
Who strive to juggle our new busy lives

We are driven by the will to achieve
And grateful for all the support we receive
The next thing to do was learning to drive
Another new challenge to take in my stride

The children left home and gone their own way
It's time to relax at the end of the day
A few foreign holidays now are the norm
Is it now time to repose and conform?

Retirement loomed but it wasn't to be
I was asked to be part of a new company
No time to take part in reflexology
Must get to grips with new technology

What strides we have made from those early years
When women of my age were considered 'old dears'
We have found new ambitions and conquered new goals
Look forward and upward and never grow old.

Margaret Adkin

My Love

My love for you flows like a river,
Forever meandering as if for a reason.
My love for you is like a spring fever,
Just waiting to burst into season.

My love for you is captured
On every tree that is in blossom.
My love for you continues to rapture,
As I hold it dear to my bosom.

My love for you is like a bird,
When they catch their food and sing.
My love for you as you have heard,
So when will you wear my ring?

My love for you was no fate,
But was grown on good friendship.
My love for you is an unlocked gate
And was sealed with my lips.

My love for you is out in the open
And flows freely in the hills.
My love for you, I write with this pen,
Is like a love story from Boon and Mills.

Naomi Sheming

The Mask

Those moments alone feeling only despair
Wondering why, when and where?
Time in solitude shared with a tear
The sadness I hide. Closeness I fear

The wall I've built hides the real me
A stranger to myself. Who is she?
Ones closest to me I push away
And yearn for another, better day

And so to sleep but peace eludes me
Dawn breaks and the world will see
The smiles and laughter all in place
Is only the mask that hides the face.

Kay Chester

THE SEPARATION

Today I won an Oscar.
My acting was so good,
I never showed emotion
Like you thought I would.

I was so cool and charming,
I never shed a tear,
Even when you packed your case
And said, 'Goodbye, my dear.'

My eyes were bright with unshed tears
I wore a painted smile
I did not show the pain within
To weep was not my style.

I watched you saunter down the path,
Your face like granite stone,
I prayed that you would not turn round,
Or hear me softly moan.

I want to shout for you to stay -
Please don't leave - don't walk away -
But these are words I cannot say
I have my pride - come what may!

Years of happiness like leaves - blown away
Care not for the heartache you've left here today.
The car door shuts and you are gone -
Goodbye my love - my only one!

Annette King

MY DAY

Patches of blue sky appear
Between the leaves on the tree
Where the sun turns them to gold
A beautiful carpet it appears to me.

A flash of white feathers
As birds wing their way
To explore the universe
On this fine autumn day.

Lying back I gaze
Out of my window, then
Closing my eyes not willing to wake
I picture the morning, decisions to make.

I hear a door bang
In the communal hall
It's Frank the postman
On his morning call.

What exciting letter for me today
Maybe a cheque but more likely a bill
Why does this sort of mail
Always happen to me?

My mail box opened
Two letters for me
No bill in sight
I'm happy to see.

One top quality envelope
From friend or foe?
I'm all of a jitter then gasp with shock
For to Buckingham Palace I'm invited to go
To Her Majesty's tea party at three o'clock.

Olive M Stout

THE FAT

I have a mind that's very intelligent
I have a heart that's pure as gold
My life is blessed with amazing friends and family
But my body is covered with dimples and folds!

You see the fat
Is a very visual thing
And I'm judged by it
Before I even begin

But that's just the kind of world we live in
Where appearance plays a major part
It doesn't matter who you truly are
Or what's really in your heart

But I'm not here to lie
And say I don't know why
Or pretend I hardly eat a thing
Or convince others I live on wind.
I know I am responsible
And the extra weight on my hips
Comes from the extra portions that pass my lips

But I don't judge you
By your thinning hair
By the size of your nose
Or your extra-marital affairs

I take you as I see you
And keep an open mind
I look for the bright and positive within you
And welcome the differences that I find.

Kiechelle Degale

ISOLATION

I need - the comfort of the written word,
The 'all-consoling' unheard of voice of script,
To be enveloped in the timeless usage of the pen
Whilst in the cup of loneliness I dip.
I need - the warmth of thoughts that stay unspoken
Embedding me; Earth's chattels cannot touch,
Surround, protect, embrace - they cannot pacify
When the sadness of this place becomes too much.
I need - the all-consuming concentrate of thought
To exclude invasive problems of this world,
To swirl sublimely in the myriads of the mind,
With pen in hand emotions are unfurled.
The need; the aim of lines that lay before me
Is to absorb - to remove me from this Earth.
The momentary soporific haze of verse
Must distance other matters of less worth.
My need, my greatest need, could I be unaware?
A void, an aching emptiness revealed.
The worries toss and tumble in the vacuum created,
Has the writing of these lines in some way healed?
I need - a kindred spirit in this world of mine,
This mental, misty, timeless, endless space,
Come - join me, fill the void and let our thoughts combine,
You are there; I hear your voice, I see your face.

J Conium

MOTHERHOOD

When you have a child, they're only yours for lends.
The way they live and learn; a lot on you depends.
So always give love freely,
Not on their feelings trample,
Surely the best way of setting a good example.

Muriel Grey

A Summer's Afternoon

Sitting in the garden on a summer's afternoon
Is a pleasure without measure for me.
With floral umbrellas and tasteful garden chairs
We rest in the shade of the laburnum tree.

Over to the left is an elegant pebble pool
With a fountain in the centre don't you know?
And then there are some statues, one of little Pan,
With his pipes up to his lips for him to blow!

Then round about 4 o'clock we like to have some tea
From fine china cups enjoy the best Earl Grey.
Our table is covered with a cloth of linen and lace
And it's all served up upon a silver tray.

Naturally, it follows, we also like to choose
From a selection of delightful fairy cakes.
Cook is awfully good to us and never makes a fuss . . .
In truth, it's me who really makes and bakes!

In actual fact we are only ordinary folk
With a pretty little garden so serene,
But sitting in that garden on a summer's afternoon
We feel just like a proper king and queen!

Margaret Brown

Untitled

Can you imagine how it feels at the age of 31
To be infertile, can life go on?
But now I have twins with the aid of IVF -
Can you believe it . . . God bless.

Gaye Jowett

A BIG REMINDER

Oh it is a busy life
Rushing to and fro
Getting nowhere fast - I think
How fast can I go

Is it worth the hassle
What do I achieve
Do I ever get there
So I like to believe

Can I get there slower
Must I always rush
What's the point of killing myself
It'll only make a fuss

Do I get acknowledged
What if I weren't there
Would they manage without me
Do they really care

Take time out to ponder
Take time out to think
Slow down now or who knows
When or where you'll sink

Stop and listen to others
Giving their advice
Think about yourself for once
They're only being nice

When you're six foot under
Will they really care
They'll fill your shoes with another
But none so big and rare

Sit down with the paper
Sit down with a bun
Sit down and remember
All the work you've done

When you're old and wrinkled
You will wonder why
Life shot by so quickly
My oh my oh my

It's time to stop this writing
As I must go to bed
Remember now stop rushing
Or you will end up dead

Rosemary Ward-Jackson

AVERAGE

An ordinary day, you might say average
If there is such a thing as average
An altogether regular you and me and here and now
If indeed you and I can be regular
Action-packed, untamed energy
Fun, instantly chaotic brilliant mess
Involved, an automatic desire to learn
The ordinary every day his guide
Imagination, dreams and desires born in the eyes of a child
Ingenious daily growth of body and mind
Learning, listening and teaching
A tiny new explorer of every average day

Sarah Murkin

FROM MY BEDROOM

I hide my dreams behind my smiles
As adventure calls, begets, beguiles.
I open my Pandora's box
Of *Tarot* cards and fresh, clean socks.

The window beckons, calls to me
To see the rainbow o'er the sea
And dolphins playing close to shore,
As wind chimes tinkle o'er the door.

The night is falling, falling fast,
Its spell of mystery to cast.
The stars will then begin their show
To call the chosen from below.

Shall I answer? Dare I to?
Where will they lead - a journey new?
What civilisations bravely sought?
What new worlds has His Holy hand wrought?

Does my quest for knowledge offend my God?
Do I blaspheme if dare I trod
To secret places man daren't know?
Will God in righteous fury show

That we mere mortals should only cringe
And keep ourselves upon the fringe?
Can it safely be assumed
That if we question, we are doomed -

Cast into Hell with no reprieve?
A point that we should surely grieve!
I'll try to avoid God's (and critic's) wrath,
But for now, I think, a nice, hot bath!

Marla Mitchell Coronel

MY TEETH

As a child, I didn't think
How much teeth cleaning meant.
I'd brush with Gibbs, at intervals
And hope I wouldn't be sent
To the clinic dentist
He was old and such a brute
He'd give you anaesthetic
And pull teeth and leave the root.

When I grew up I cherished my white teeth,
A full compliment of them,
I went and changed my dentist
And he took care of them.
He'd clean and polish in my mouth
Do a filling, maybe two
I'd visit him twice yearly
At almost seventy, I still do.

I've lost a molar here and there,
Through abscesses at the root
It must have been heredity
Cos Dad had all his out.
I'm looking after these that's left
And clean with power brush
I can still bite apples
And my food is far from mush.

So my white teeth I still cherish
All twenty-five of them,
And I hope that I still have them
When they take me to the *Crem.*

Elizabeth Stevens

WHAT'S A MOTHER FOR?

Take the dog out
Mow the lawn
Wipe the kitchen wall
Wash a pile of dishes
Gather clothes thrown in the hall
Make the bed
Hoover around
Pick up the clothes to wash
Put his shoes away from under the bed
And clean the bath and bosh
Run to town to fetch the shop
Collect the kids from school
Must rush home
Iron his shirt for it's his night for playing pool
At last it's quiet, all in bed
Let the dog out, shut the garden gate
It's 11 o'clock he'll soon be home
Better put his sandwiches on the plate
I sometimes dream of 9 till 5
Dressed up each day, what a life
But there's no redundancies in my job
Because I'm a mother and a wife!

Margaret Davies

MISSING YOU

My heart deflates and I feel very sick
It's just after you've gone through the door.
I then try and wish the day away,
So I can kiss and hold you once more.

I can't help having these feelings my love
It's because I hold you so dear
You're the light in my dark and
The only one to execute my fears.

You are strong and lively and a little loud
But the house is now very still
You go out and let desolation in
And my eyes are beginning to fill.

The gap you leave is just too wide
I'm struggling to cope
I just wish we never had to part
Oh, this woman is full of hope!

Wendy Jane Langton

WHAT A SILLY STATISTIC

What a silly statistic
It has nothing to do with me
And if what they say is true
I'll be one of the other three

What a silly statistic
To say that he's beaten me
He has such a gentle nature
Surely you must agree

What a silly statistic
He may be causing me pain
He doesn't mean to hurt me
He just can't seem to refrain

What a silly statistic
I feel I must hide my pain
Because he's always so ashamed
And promises never again

What a silly statistic
Why are you staring at me?
I always wear lots of make-up
I've nothing to hide you see

Judith Gillham

PEACE OF MIND

Children grown and moved away, families of their own to raise,
love to see them when I can, but wish the journey wasn't so bad.
Retirement age looms very near, is this really such a good idea?
What will I do when home all day, partner still with years to stay,
in the job where he spends his waking hours, with a woman for
whom he often buys flowers.

I seem to tire so easily, yet when in bed I cannot sleep.
The hours tick by, my thoughts won't stop, panic sets in and
my mind runs amok.
When at last I drop off I have frightening dreams, the alarm goes
off and I'm almost relieved, but even more tired than before it seems.

So off to work where the day is fraught, at least it's better than home
with my thoughts.
Do I have the courage to start again, the options are there, but where
and when?
Is the grass greener on the other side and would being alone be worth
peace of mind?

This getting old is not much fun, where did all my confidence go?
I used to be so sure of things, but now I live from day to day,
hoping these feelings will go away.
Perhaps they will and life will get better, but I hope it's soon as I feel
so down, where could I go for a night on the town?

The world is fun if you're under thirty, but not if you're fifty and
feeling flirty.
Among the young I'd just look sad and remind me of the energy
I once had.
You're supposed to grow old gracefully, but who wants to grow old -
even tastefully?

Jean Walker

MEN

I'm glad I'm a woman and not a man, a man thinks he might,
a woman knows she can.
While a woman gets cracking and gets things done, a man's
first thought is having fun!
A man takes a woman to be his wife and thinks he has a slave for life.
She bears his children and cooks his meals, yet he hasn't a clue
about the way she feels.
Most men I know have got big feet, I like a man who is tidy and neat.
As they get older and the whiskers grow, the bald bit on top begins
to show.
He thinks cooking and cleaning are just child's play, while he has
been out at work all day.
At weekends it's football down at the club, then one or two pints
down at the pub.
He will argue that men are the superior gender, but what are they like
when they have been on a bender?
All the excuses that they can muster, with slurring speech and all
that bluster.
Then sleeping it off with whistle and snore and dirty clothes all
over the floor.
A woman's work is never done, yet I confess I'm the lucky one.
I'm not only a wife, but a mother of three and that's hard work,
any woman would agree.
I'm grateful for the blessings that I have had, each one a lovely
little *lad*.
Am I glad that I'm a woman and not a man? I can honestly
and truthfully say that I am.

Patricia Thirlby

Mummy... Where Did I Come From?

'Mummy . . . where did I come from?' Asked Caitlin,
freshly tucked in her bed,
Lesley flushed red with excitement, hearing the question
that all parents dread.
'It's late, you really must sleep now,' said Lesley, to try to delay
'You'll have to be up early tomorrow, but I promise I'll tell you
one day.'

'But Mummy my teacher has asked me, she says that I really
should know,
I promised I'd tell her tomorrow, if I don't know, I don't think I'll go!'
Tucking her head under her pillow and kicking poor Ted out of bed,
She slipped down the sheets in an instant and she wouldn't when asked,
raise her head.

Oh why couldn't Christian be here now! And not with his mates down
the pub!
I'll cut off all his shirt buttons; and the dog can put pay to his grub!
'Oh, alright, sit up and I'll tell you, about the birds and the bees.'
And slowly she felt her young daughter; arch her back as she got
to her knees.

Lesley started to sweat and to stutter, as she nervously began to relate,
How love can bring about babies and how various animals mate.
Her daughter sat silent and listened and looked at her mum quite
perplexed,
As the sweat on her mum's forehead glistened, as she pondered what
wonders
came next.

Feeling rightfully proud of her answer and for keeping such a clear head
She had stopped the prancing and pacing and sat herself down
on the bed.
She then bade her daughter to sleep now, as she kissed little Caitlin
goodnight,
After returning poor Ted to his slumber, in the faintest glimmer of light.

Lesley walked towards the doorway, she hadn't moved that far,
And grabbed the handle firmly, on the door which stood half ajar.
It was then that Caitlin shouted, 'But Mummy I don't understand!
Malika's just started in our class and she comes from Pakistan!'

Linda Billington

REMEMBERING

Another year has passed and doesn't time fly?
But each day you remain in my thoughts
and as the seasons of the year changes
I think of the joy in the past you had brought

And since you have passed
each day has never been the same
and sometimes tears will sting my eyes
and still I feel your death, has been in vain.

The pain has eased a little but I know that is fine,
because since you have gone
I have learned that in life we must do our best
and when the bad times strike so suddenly
it is to put us to the test of:
are we humble, are we strong
do we know the rights from wrongs?
Are we patient, are we kind
do we give others less fortunate some of our time?

I am not ashamed to say that I sometimes sit and cry
and shake my head and sigh and wonder *why*
and here I am *remembering* memories of you
and memories of mine
coasting along slowly, sometimes carefully

through this passage of time.

Micky-Ives

FREEDOM

Oh to be free. Free as the bird in the sky,
Released from the pain of living a lie.
No end in sight, trapped in darkness and fear.
Each new lie becomes but another tear.
How I wish I could fly up, up and away,
Just like a bird, with nothing to worry about.
No more tears or wanting out loud to shout.
No more can one do, there's nothing else to say.
Oh to be free, free to soar up so high
Just like that bird winging its way to the sky
With peace in my heart and joy in my sight
Like that bird I want to be free,
Heading into the sun and over the sea.
No pain, no more battles to fight,
Freedom to be that bird on the wing
With nothing to do, but swoop and sing.

Jennifer Walsh

OLD AGE

Don't look at me old and grey
My face lined from many a day
Don't turn around when I try to speak
I may have the knowledge you seek
You may have youth and beauty on view
But I have more experience than you
I would not speak over and over again
If I spoke more often to keep me sane
I would love to share your laughter and fun
But you turn away, because you think I am done.

C Bartholomew

FIRST HOUR

One hour before the school bell rings,
Cleaning up the breakfast things,
Two kids fighting in next room
Hardly time to just vacuum.
TV on much too loud!
Cat miaows for its food.
Not much time the clock is ticking
Little one starts the usual kicking.
The big one says he's not going
That cat just keeps on miaowing.
Washer's on and dryer's spinning
I really think I'm not winning.
Out the house we rush along
Big one starts to sing a song.
He makes me smile, pressure's off!
Once again we beat the clock.

A A Brown

UNTIL YOU

Before I met you
I never knew
You existed
I never knew
A person could
Shine so bright
Bring so much joy
Shoulder so much pain
Until I knew you
And then
I couldn't get you
Out of my head.

Michelle Penny

OFFSPRING

Into the world as babes you come, defenceless, helpless, new,
Dependant on your parents' love to guide and see you through.
Suckled, bathed, dressed in white, the pride of parents who . . .
Give up the best of twenty years to raising only you.

Sleepless nights with countless feeds, you wake at least three times!
She walks the floor in dead of night, as lonely church bell rings.
Then comes the morn, so bright and new, a fresh day starts again,
The feeding, bathing, changing needs near drive your mum insane.

But time rolls by, months and years and you begin to grow,
We see the pleasure in your eyes . . . your parents love you so.
Your every need is met by them, they give you all . . . and more,
Great hopes they have for you, their child,
                          as through young life you soar.

With letters, words and numbers too, they help to build your mind,
Attending to your every need . . . attentive, loving, kind.
You're fed and clothed . . . no matter what . . .
                          some days they go without
To give you all the things they missed, but you won't hear them grouch.

Through education now you've gone, apprentice . . . now you are,
And pride of place in parents' hearts, their offspring will go far.
The years have flown . . . now they are old, their duty . . . nearly done,
They gave their love, their lives, their hearts, for their ever loving son.

Gloria Courts

JIGSAW WOMAN

She carefully lifted the fragments, one by one,
Shards of my former self -
Once a fully jointed, fully working model,
Hinges all rusted and disabled now
By the tortured stretch to escape this mindish grief.

She took them up so very gently, one by one,
And put me together again.
I ache to stay within that close embrace,
Of honest love, of sister love,
That didn't ask for when, for how long,
But just endures forever.

Anna K V Hallam

ALL OF TIME
(Dedicated to my wonderful boyfriend Simon Cox)

Feeling lost, afraid and alone,
In this cold wilderness of life
Scared to love and scared to cry
I don't want anyone to see how much I hurt inside.
Afraid to be loved and afraid to be held
Frightened to surrender
To the feeling deep inside
Needing a friend, wanting so much more
Hoping he is the one
Who can light my path
Through the darkness and pain of the world.
Afraid to trust in love
For fear of being hurt
Scared to show how I really feel
In case I'm pushed away
Afraid to tell the truth
Of how deep my feelings go
A love in truth, a love be told
And a love I could never forsake.
A winding river never flows off course
But keeps true to the ocean.
He's an angel in my eyes
My love for all time.

Shèle K Martin

ALONE HOME

I ask you, can you picture it now, the bleak, gloomy setting.
Dull sky with half a moon rising above the architecture
Sitting proud on the hill so regal and bold.
Oh! But so very old this empty house a cold hearth it does behold.

Well it sounds dramatic, but the truth you would not believe.
You see I am that lonely house, that lone home, home alone!
And the boldest thing about my architecture is my smoke-blackened chimney;
But even that isn't so bold because all the others in the street look the same.
Did you ever think that sameness could make you feel so lonely.

A lovely row of terraced houses all looking the same.
When we were built we were a housing revolution,
Steel girders and reinforced concrete,
All constructed together eight, nine sometimes ten in a row,
A little garden at the front, neat backyards for the families to come and go
And the children to play or some flowers to grow.

But the times have changed and people moved on,
No more families to-ing and fro-ing all the good times have gone.
It's the Housing Executive that I hold to blame with their men in grey suits, big official folders and strategic housing plans.
To help make this nation a neat and tidy land compatible neighbours they did uproot
In their bid for *segregation* the new buzz word in government walls.

Fear and isolation seeped in as Old Ireland's wars and rebellions found new ground in which to breed.
On the streets of our fast track estates came mini rival gangs full of destruction, boredom and teenage angst!
One by one our windows were blasted to smithereens, our doors bashed in,
Our gardens saw the scenes of mass destruction, where many an innocent head was kicked in.

So now here I stand . . . alone in this row,
My gaping windows boarded up with metal grids
Blinking wide like two blackened eyes.
We're doomed for demolition sometime soon wouldn't you know
An architect's dream crushed down like slushy, melting snow.

Lorna M Gough

NON-SEXIST

I'm a non-sexist tomboy, fitness freak,
My aim each day is quite clear,
Equality is my only watchword,
And winning I always hold dear.
I drive a big tractor, work hard for my pay,
Compete, put my skills to the test,
I can plough a straight furrow, lay a fine hedge,
Men know that my work is no jest!
Assault course training is part of my life,
I now have my wings and can fly,
White water rafting my absolute joy,
I should have been born a strong boy!
Harness racing, a positive must,
Indeed danger and speed and a fight,
Onlookers know that I'll give all I've got,
I'll tear round the track with my might.
One day a jockey with bold eye and shrewd,
Whom I'd known now for many a year,
Gave me the latest race of my life,
When he asked me to marry and thus be his wife!
A non-sexist girl to the end I will be,
Both sexes are equal and beautifully free;
So why have I ended up bearing his child,
Washing his shirts and now cooking for three?

Norma Rudge

HOPEFULLY OUT OF THE TEARS COMES A SMILE

Our Ellen and Dennis were a special pair, they lived their lives
                                                            to the full,
They travelled here, they travelled there, but their lives were
                                                            never dull.

Now start at the beginning as I remember years ago
She met her Dennis and fell in love and she became his beau.
I remember they lived in Spondon with Dennis' mum and dad
They eventually got a council house that made them very glad.
They had a little boy called Steve and he was a little devil
So they bunged him in the army before he became a rebel.
And then they had a little girl, and decided to call her Sue
She was a massive baby though, just all of 10lb 2.
'Don't have any more kids,' the doctors said,
'So Dennis, tie a knot in it, before you go to bed.'
Climbing into bed each night and wanting a bit of the other
'You know what you can do our Den, you can go and live
                                                        with your mother.'
Dennis wandered down life's highway looking all forlorn
I've had enough of all of this I'm retiring to Eastbourne.

We had some great times by the sea but it wasn't long for sure
My life was taken away from me and I was only 64!

'Ellen, I'm sitting cross-legged on a cloud wondering what to do!
I know I'll paint a rainbow and send it just for you.
Next time you see a cloudy sky peeping through the blue
I'll give you a smile and then a wave, it's just to say *I love you.*
When your time comes in later life and you're wondering what is what
Don't worry my gal, I'll see you alright
Cause *guess what*? I've just managed to undo that bloody knot!'

Maggie Lakin

THE FINAL CURTAIN

She lifted her tired body from the tousled bed
Every ache and pain attacked her simultaneously
Her head throbbing, causing shock rays across her eyes
Her body was completely dysfunctional.

For the last fifty-four years she had risen from her bed
Her sole mission to make her way to work
To earn her living day by day
And with her life the price to pay.

It had been her ambition in her youth
To make her money and run, so to speak
To retire at a very early age
Leaving plenty of time to enjoy life to the full.

Looking back it had not been like that
She had not claimed control of her own life
Everybody had made their drastic demands on it
Until she was left alone, a shadow of her former self.

Everyone close to her had passed on
She had nursed them until the end
There had been many suitors but they had now gone
Refusing to wait until she felt free from her obligations.

She tried to step out of her bed, her legs refused to move
Wait! What was her mother doing here and her father too?
Suddenly the numbness alleviated and without any help on her part
She floated from the bed, encased in an aura of shining gold
She knew all was well, eternal peace was hers.

Irene H Gabriel

A Woman's World

Below us there are burning coals,
A central core under our feet
And when I think of just how long
Our molten world has made that heat,
I'm just a flame amongst the pyre,
A lonely spark but growing higher
As many flames become a fire.

Around us are the endless seas,
So deep the light just can't shine through
And when it rains, each single drop
Reminds me of what's really true.
I'm just a little piece of sea,
I'm less than what I thought I'd be
But tidal waves are made by me.

Above us are as many stars
As grains of sand upon the earth.
To try and think of such a thing
Gives me a sense of my own worth.
I'm just a sparkle in the night,
I'm just a single spot of light
But made of fire I'm burning bright.

Andrea K Ellis

Isabel

What can I say about Isabel,
The new little girl in our lives.
With her chubby cheeks and pretty mouth
And her sparkling denim blue eyes.

She talks a lot of rubbish,
She sings to us as well.
Her smile is quite delightful,
We're completely under her spell.

May her days be always sunny
And love and care abound.
Good luck, good health and laughter,
Our Isabel surround.

Kathleen McGuinness

LONELINESS

I lie awake -
It's midnight -
I'm on my own - alone
What happened to my dreams in life?
My family - my home?

The body's tired, the mind's alert
The hard day's work numbs out the hurt.
Our 'grown up' children are out to play . . .
They live night lives and sleep by day!
Their lives are full of hopes and dreams,
A fantasy of life it seems.
For in reality all we need,
Has been devoured by simple greed.
The money's earnt to pay the bills
And more money spent to 'ring the tills'.
We work, we slave, to do our best
But when does time give us a rest?
My other half, he works by night
To earn some more to see us right!
But where's the time to stop and say
The things that matter every day?

A glass of wine has made me sleepy.
The book I read has made me weepy.
Another day has now passed by.
I switch out the light and alone I lie.

Glenda Melluish

I MUST GET A BODY

Just one more set girls.
March, march, march, march.
It's quick,
Give me a triceps stretch, a biceps curl.
And give me a press.
One two three.
Arms out, arms in, arms up, arms under.
One two three knee.
One two three knee.
And take a drink on board.
Grab some weights.
Bow and arrow, bow and arrow.
And give me a squat, clap.
Squat clap, squat clap.
You can do it.
Everybody happy?
Split stance,
Pulse, pulse, pulse, pulse.

Control it, control it.
Take a drink on board.
Grab your mats.
Press-ups.
One two three up,
One two three down.
Remember the breathing.
In out, in out.
Core strength, think core strength.
Just one more set girls.
All I wanted was a body not to join the bloody SAS.
Just one more set girls.

Senga Wallace Roche

OLDER WOMAN DRIVER

What is this, God?
I set out early,
Tank full,
At the crack of egg;
The big hand was on seven
And the little one on twelve -
You were in your heaven,
Et cetera, et cetera -
And now it seems
The dials were all set wrong
From the beginning.

Hey there, God!
You in the machine,
I thought I had 10,000 miles' worth
Under my bonnet
But the needle's going down,
The sunshine roof is closing
And the clock's gone back.
(As the vicar said,
'Winter draws on.')

Now of my whatever-score-years-and-ten,
Too many will not come again.
So much for British summertime -
Here today and gone tomorrow.
It's God's time now
That is measuring my length.

So -
What is this, God?
Is this red light
The setting sun in my eyes,
Or am I running on *empty?*

Judith M Warrington

TIME TO LET GO

Our terraced house seemed once too small,
Now too much space from wall to wall,
You've all left home and gone your ways,
There is nothing left but empty days,
I walk around from room to room,
My heart is empty, full of gloom.

Sunday is my special day,
I hear your voices from far away,
I love and miss you more each day,
The price a mum just has to pay,
I always knew one day you'd go,
I didn't think it would hurt so.

It's selfish now to want you home,
The time has come for us to roam,
Take ourselves to foreign places,
Meet new friends and see new faces,
One last thought where'er we be,
You can't cut down our family tree!

Margaret Longcake

WHY DO YOU LOOK AT ME LIKE THAT?

Why do you look at me like that, I've only got a scarf on,
My skin is pink, I have two legs
My arms move, my eyes blink,
So why do you stare, stranger?
Is it because you care, or are you scared?

Why do you look at me like that, I haven't lost my mind,
I can still hold a conversation, try me
I am in charge of all my faculties and my bodily functions,
So why do you stare stranger are you curious or relieved.
Or have you never seen a woman in a scarf?

I think I know the reason why you stare,
I think you know I have a disease that you or I could share,
I think you are glad it is not you, stranger,
But don't be complacent a few short months ago,
I was just like you too, I didn't need to wear a scarf either.

Catherine Taylor

A Carer's Cry

'Hi Mum, hi Dad, how are you today?'
My smiling mask makes you think I'm okay.

Day in, week out,
Another year of grey,
Where do they get their strength?
From wearing mine away?

At 55 will I ever be free,
To do what I want
And be who I desperately need to be?
What is awaiting me?

The family have flown,
The marriage tires,
The mask says 'I'm fine',
The heart feels desires.

I restart the clock and dream,
Travel, career, time to relax,
Could that have been me?
Perhaps, perhaps.

Hi Mum, hi Dad, how are you today?

Rita E Lewis

OPENING DAY AT GUNWHARF QUAYS

Today 28th February, 2001,
As soon as we'd eaten our lunch at home in Southsea we were gone,
Dashing to Portsmouth Harbour to the newly opened Gunwharf Quays,
I knew it would come up to all our expectations so would please,
Apparently there were, I think, about ten thousand people there,
I believe there is nothing else on the south coast to quite compare,
Four million people a year this may bring into our city,
The cinema and bowling will provide leisure activity,
Gunwharf Quays has the largest underground car park in the UK,
We wouldn't have missed going to Gunwharf on the opening day,
For nearly seven years we've waited for this, it's so exciting,
It will be an unrivalled waterfront complex nice and bustling,
In the summertime there will be ocean-going yachts and tall ships
Tied up on the waterfront, it all will look good from Blue Boat trips
As well as from the restaurants, there's plenty of eating places -
Coffee bars, cafes, pubs, nice to see so many happy faces,
Discount and factory shops give a new shopping experience,
The various buildings and malls looked splendid through my
                                                                camera lens,
There is a variety of shops, about forty were open,
We will visit Gunwharf Quays again and I know exactly when -
In three days time when we will see the market and entertainment,
We bought some coffee, chocolate and biscuits, it was money
                                                                         well spent,
At Easter maybe more shops will be open, we will go again,
Near the entrance there are bridges, a weir, a crane and a fountain,
We can't wait to browse round the market which will be there
                                                                        all weekend,
A few hours looking, buying amongst crowds will be nice to spend,
The carnival on Sunday will make an electric atmosphere,
To the attractive Gunwharf Quays we are lucky to live so near.

Gill Coombes

HAPPY EVER AFTER

We moved in together, it was like a dream,
I glowed from ear to ear, the cat that got the cream.
We had a big wedding, a fairytale day,
Honeymooned abroad, wished that we could stay.

But then the bubble burst, the nightmare began,
My darling honey bun became the Neanderthal man.
Mine's tea with two sugars and make it snappy,
It was only three months, I was less than happy.

Dirty football socks and beer-stained shirts,
Subjected to The Doves now that really hurts.
PlayStation games all over my lounge floor,
My hunky bit of stuff was becoming a real bore.

Asked my mum, 'Is this what married life's about?'
'It'll get worse before it gets better,' she had no doubt.
So I got on with it and things, I thought got better.
But then I found it, that perfume-sprayed letter.

'I really love you Johnny, wish you'd leave your wife.
I'm sure we'd be happy and have a great sex life.'
I was numb with shock, my John had been untrue,
I should have seen the signs, but didn't have a clue.

Course he said she meant nothing and never had,
Didn't show much sympathy for saying I was so sad.
Went out to the pub and left me alone,
Rang up my pal, spent the night on the phone.

So the dream is over I've given him the boot,
Gave up on the loser in the designer suit.
So I'm single again, no men in my life,
Back to square one, but at least I've got no strife.

Sally Yeomans

Alone In The Large, Cold Bathroom

All alone in that large, silent, cold bathroom,
naked and suddenly aware,
An awareness of my naked body, soft flesh, the body hair.
How long had it been since I last looked, aware of my naked flesh?
The sudden realisation that I had breasts, arms, legs. It was fresh.
How long since I had looked at my body? For too long I had not dare.

So long I had covered up my bare flesh, I had been hiding it away,
I hid from the world, from myself;
Keeping what I had grown to hate at bay.
So long I had resented this damaged body,
this full length naked human being,
I did not want to see what had been examined again and again
hoping to find something.
Awareness grew, how I had not wanted to look into the
full length mirror that day.

I stood silent, naked, staring at myself, how I hated it so much,
A body I often wished was not mine, I had so long denied my body
a tender touch.
Why? So long, so long it had been examined, pressed, prodded
by medical strangers,
Doing their job, I know to diagnose to avoid potential dangers.
So long . . . I had not looked, I had not felt; I just resented it so much.

Marie-Louise McCormick

Separation

From the moment I was pregnant
I knew I'd rue the day
When you'd become young adolescents
And would start to branch away.

I knew I'd feel lost without you
Incomplete - a trifle bored
I didn't expect it to be so painful though
This cutting of the cord.

Pauline Scrivener

AN ODE TO MOTHERHOOD

Be there when I need you
But go when I don't.
Just tell me to do it,
You know that I won't.

I've grown up at last,
I'm an adult you see,
So get off my back
And just let me be.

The wide world is beckoning,
I'm filled with such glee,
With you to finance me,
I'll see it for free!

Don't worry dear parents
You know I'm all right,
Don't give me a thought
As you turn out the light.

I've grown up and gone
And now you are free.
Why don't you invite
All your friends round for tea.

What's that dear Mother,
My room is not free?
But that is my home,
That room is for me!

Sue Lowe

MOST THINGS ARE ROTTEN

Sugar and spice and all things nice.

'Sugar,' he said, leaning across the bar,
His breath rotten with alcohol,
Fermenting the air around him.
'Those eyes are sapphires . . . did your dad steal them?'
An eloquent courting phrase,
Romantic poetry,
This Shakespeare is going home alone.

Sugar and spice and all things nice.

'Spice up your love life?' he gestured
To the bulge in his trousers,
Jeering to his mates and winking at me.
'I can tell what you're into alright!'
An acute psychic,
A clairvoyant courier,
It appears this soothsayer, is wrong.

Sugar and spice and all things nice.

'Nice arse,' he yelled, hanging limply
From his machine, scratching his sand-paper face,
Like a monkey hanging from a tree.
'You can ride my bulldozer any day!'
A complaisant invitation,
An idyllic request,
It seems this uninviting host has no one at his party.

Sugar and spice,
Things aren't always nice,
All things nice,
Only come with a price,
Often forgotten:
Most things are rotten.

Jessica Moody

MUM

Mum, do you think I'm growing up?
I heard something funny from a friend,
Her 16 year old daughter is driving her nuts,
And she thinks it will never end.

I want to tell her, wait for it,
The best years are yet to come,
It's when you change - the both of you,
And your best friend becomes your mum.

It suddenly made me think of us,
I know we've been there too,
And I'm sure you will remember,
Some of the troubles that I caused you!

My growing years, my problems,
I know I've raised a few,
But *never* once have you doubted me,
And that's because you're *you!*

The times we're apart, I miss you,
Our talks, our laughs, our love,
You'll never change, my mother,
And for that I'm grateful of.

But now, the times we share together,
When we're really on our own,
Are the ones that I appreciate,
You're the best friend I've ever known.

Mum, it's hard to put it into words,
No card I find will say,
That your precious love and friendship
Is locked in my heart - *to stay.*

Beth Windsor

MY MOTHER

All that I hate
I held inside,
I kept it tight
Until she died.

She went off
With someone new,
Left us girls,
Wrote letters few.

Big parcels came
Again and again,
But, no parcel
Would take the pain.

My sisters didn't
Seem to care,
But all the pain
I couldn't bear.

I tried so hard
To understand
Why she left us
For a man.

We weren't that bad,
Just normal girls,
Not fancy, no frills,
Not even any curls.

Gran and Ding
Did their best,
Cheques arrived and
We were dressed.

Good food, nice home,
Always clean and tidy,
Credit to 'our' mum,
But she was in hiding.

My sisters didn't
Seem to care,
All this pain
I still can't bear.

Charmaine Edwards

KISSES

I have forgotten how
we kissed.
Is that it gone?
The memories of
your tongue,
your taste,
your smile.
I do remember,
but it is enclosed
within a small space
to compress the pain,
to beat the knowledge
that it is gone
and we have to
live a very different life.

The ache for your mouth
as I run my tongue
over my lips
tasting myself,
trying to remember,
makes me
shiver.

Carol S Fenelon

CARDBOARD CITY

Glistening pavements, dark thunderclouds
Scurrying footsteps, homeward-bound crowds
With lowered heads, and averted eye
They pretend we're not here and pass us by
Darkness has fallen, time for a rest
Cardboard City is my new address

Crawl into my box, hungry and damp
Read an old paper by the street lamp
Life was hard when my dad walked out
I didn't mean to swear and shout
But nobody wanted me around
And so I left, London bound

Feeling fearless, brave and bold
But now I'm tired and freezing cold
I long for a bed, a blanket, a sheet
But all I have is a dirty street
I've cut my hair to look like a lad
If Dad could see it I think he'd be sad

He used to ruffle my silky hair
But now there isn't a soul to care
How did everything go so wrong
I was fit, healthy and strong
I lost my way as so many do
In this year of 2002

E M Clowes

UNTITLED

Blot my copybook
(gunslinging)
Take me on, rubbercheeks
Lose yourself in my foolish dreams.

Move too close
Discard the outer wrapping
(overwhelm)
Freeze over the contents immediately on opening.

Elizabeth M Pritchard

BITTER WINDS

As spring survives through the winter storms,
It brings joy with blossoms on trees.
Sweet magnolias scent the air
Meadows sleep in serenity.

Yet this soul yearns
As spring can bring no more
Than the bleakness of a ravaged heart.
The wrath swells, how scornfully.

Summer takes her first breath
Glistening fields with shades of green.
Reveries bathe the evening sun,
Lost in the absence of mind
Mosquitoes dance the night away.

The coldness of the moon
Brings autumn near,
Clouds shower with tormenting tears
As winter comes without a call.

Scattered pearls glance the ebony sky,
Painting Earth with ivory white
Forever thoughts come to closure.

A silent wail, nature grieves,
Lovers drift a distant wind
Illusion fades, dusk awakes.

Runa Begum

SCHEDULES

Business Class to London, then a trip to Tokyo,
I must review the Middle East
Not sure how it'll go.
Brussels is fine (but for bureaucrats). It all takes so much time!
At least I run my own show now. The final word is mine.

New business deals
More aeroplane meals
I love my job, my life.
The buzz I get
The men I've met
No time to be a wife!

It will pan out just as I'd planned, this fantastic career
I've come so far and worked so hard, no holiday this year.
I'm ruthless, do not suffer fools, can challenge any man.
My clothes, my attitude, all say, 'Here's one who can'.

I'm proud to be
Successful. Me.
Kids aren't on my agenda.
My sister breeds
With leporid ease
I cannot comprehend her.

My life is mine why should I worry? I don't give a damn!
My bank accounts are my best friends,
They love me as I am.
No wedding bells,
No infant smells,
The jet-set life's for me.
I'll have a gin
As I begin
My flight to Helsinki!

Margaret Paxton

ALL THESE YEARS ON...

I've just finished cleaning the box room,
And now all the cupboards are bare
The posters came down and the music has stopped,
And I don't want to go back in there.

How messy it was when they lived here,
Clothes, books and junk all on the floor
And drawers spilling over with treasures,
How I wish it were like it once more.

The school trips, report cards, exam times,
All the worry, the joy and the pain
Of being an ordinary busy mum,
How on earth did I ever stay sane?

With picnics, and walks and bike rides
And many fine days by the sea,
Oh, how we cried the day 'Casper' died,
And we buried him under the tree.

So soon they were teens, and quite trying
As they sorted their identities,
Wearing funky new clothes and weird hairdos,
They could study *and* party with ease!

So now, though my nest is quite empty,
I have many fond memories, and it's clear
That I know in my heart my time's been well spent,
As worthwhile as any career.

So all these years on and I sit here
Remembering the times we had fun,
And I know that in the next day or two
I'll answer the phone to 'Hi Mum'!

Jill Gunter

MOVING ON

I'm moving onto another town
Never lived there before
A new job
A new life
A new man
Will I be protected or abused?
Will I be loved or hated?
Will I be raised up or brought down?
Will I be accepted as a person or be treated like a slave?
Will he stay with me or ditch me?
Is there hope or despair?
Will he be kind or cruel?
Will he be soft or hard?
Does he know I'm a person
Or will he see me as an object?
Oh a new job, new home, new life, new man
And still so much on my own
For I have no new friends.

Rosemary Sheehan

UNTITLED...

I made you such a part of my life,
wherever you went I would follow,
but then came the time you said goodbye
and left a part of me hollow.

And now that so much time has passed
precious memories are fading away,
however the few that still remain,
help see me through another day.

Each detail of your face in my mind,
stays with me every day,
but if we were to meet again
would we have anything to say?

If I have one regret in this life,
it is how things turned so sour.
I want to kick and scream and shout,
'cause that was my darkest hour.

Donna Drew

A ROUND TUIT

Can anybody help me?
Can you tell me where to go,
To buy a thing my husband needs,
I've searched both high and low.
The hardware store, the chemist,
They sadly shake their heads.
'Can you describe it?' they all ask,
Well I only know it's round,
And to do the jobs I'm waiting for,
One really must be found.
To mend the fence,
To paint the house,
A hundred other tasks.
It can't be anything a woman needs,
If it needs doing, we just do it,
But before a man can do a job
He needs to get a round tuit.

Jean Nutt

LOVE FREES

How easy it is to shame and blame
Those others outside - it is a mere game
I play to hide those parts of me
I choose to bind and never free
Into the light of love to merge
And heal - until one day there was an urge
To take those parts - to make a start
In freeing my shadow, allowing the heart
To love both dark and light in me
In others too, now I could see
The best in them - that was a start
A turnaround - from head to heart

Now, I know when I look at my man
With deep compassion and love - I can
Know that what I judged in him
Was my reflection - now real dim
And distant - a fading aspect of the past
I've got the message here at last
When I give love so bold and free
It flows through him - returns to me

Gina Bowman

HOLIDAY IN KOREA

Holiday time is with us again,
Should it be Austria, France or Spain?
At last it's settled, Korea calls,
With scenic blue peaks and waterfalls.

Oh what an exciting place to be,
Where rice is served for dinner and tea,
Set out on papsangs in little bowls,
Together with soup and no bread rolls.

But plenty to choose from none the less
Spare ribs, kimchi, pulgogi and cress,
Shoals of fish, served in delicate ways,
Followed by fresh fruit, served up on trays.

The shops are exciting, the markets are fun,
So much to see in the glorious sun,
Temples and parks and magnificent lakes,
And deliciously scrumptious moon festival cakes!

Violet Beattie

BUTTERFLY

With a tremor of its wafer wing
They say, a butterfly in Beijing
Can, in time, spin a tornado
Across the Kansas plain
Or hurl a tidal wave booming
Into Carolina's tranquil bays.

So, what then of a kiss for the dying
An embrace for the untouched
Or a tenderness to the crushed?

>   What of a whisper of grace,
>   A word of love unfurled
>   Or a door to truth flung wide?

Will not these unwind the twisted heart
And still the waves of endless whys?
Is this not the fountain spray
>   That soars through time
>   And splashes eternity into my eyes?

Judy Studd

GIVE IT TIME

I know that this is a crazy world, and I know that this life is cruel,
But hold on tight to what you have got and don't let yourself fall.
As I look into your eyes, I can see your pain,
I know how you are feeling, because I used to feel the same.
But I can see your future and it is looking fine,
So please don't hate yourself, and give this life some time.
Please don't hate yourself; don't hate at all,
I am here to catch you, if you ever fall.
I have felt the same pain and I know that it is hard to do,
But I will be your good friend, and try to help you through.
So don't let me see you crying, don't let me see you feeling sad,
Because out of all the people in this world, you are the best friend
                                                                  I have ever had.
And I can see your future, and it is looking fine,
But if you ever need a shelter, you can use this heart of mine.
So hold on tight to what you have got, and make it to the end,
I will always be here for you; I will always be your friend.

Maria Cope

THIS WOMAN'S LIFE

It seems so long ago when I said 'I do'.
Life changed me from a child to a woman
In such a short time we grew so far apart
Looking back, we had little left in common.

Years passed by then I met another
Yes, it felt like love but I did discover
Quite soon another patch on my heart was in tact
But now I am a mother (my happiest fact).

Life is not that long, grasp every chance
To make happy days and enjoy romance
As today's woman I am wiser (a lesson learned well)
I just got back up there after I had stumbled and fell.

Now, as fifty approaches and my grandchildren grow
Love and peace live life with me, that I now know
I came through the dark, found the man that I love
Now my life is in hand and fits like a glove.

Jo Hodson

GO QUIETLY

Sleep soundly with the happiest of dreams,
Awake to sunlight kissing with her golden beams,
Go quietly into every newborn day,
Marvelling at nature and her beautiful display.

Tread softly lest you wake a nesting bird,
Come glow of dawn, then her sweetest song is heard.
Speak in whispers as you slowly pass them by,
Lest they flee and vanish away into the sky.

Spread love and caring as you travel through each day,
Making many friends as you pass upon your way.
Offer a helping hand to all you meet in need,
Never hesitating to perform the kindest deed.

When day is done and you return home, tired and worn,
Rest in peace on thy pillow until arrives a new dawn.

Peggy Millie Allan

PRETENCE

Now I've turned thirty, time sure does fly,
I've caught a few moments of the day passing by,
To sit and to wonder what thoughts lay inside,
What memories stir me, what feelings I hide.

A family home with a study, dishwasher too,
And one day we'll turn one car into two.
But it's all for show, and our friends they don't see,
That we are not always what we seem to be.

Loan upon loan have been signed up for years,
I'm thinking too much, now start the tears.
The pressures are constantly looming their head,
Do I have enough cash to buy some more bread?

The catalogues scream, pay up, your bills due,
Electric and gas and the telephone too.
We talk of a budget to ease all the strain,
What else can we do to avert all this pain?

The price that we pay for our house and our car,
Is it really worth slaving to get us this far?
All the travelling to do, hours spent on the train,
Early mornings to work, cycling home in the rain.

Just keep it together and we will survive,
We'll hold onto each other and keep love alive.
Then one day will come when the seas will be calmer,
And we'll remember the days when the summers were warmer.

We'll remember the girls fighting over a toy
And look back with emotion at the birth of our boy.
It is worth the work and accounts in the red,
For what we are building is not just in our head.

It's a future for all of our family to hold,
A life to look back on when we are both old.
But I'll keep the pretence to all of my friends,
And tomorrow I'll shop and money I'll lend.

Elaine Rogers

MY PRIVILEGE

I always wished when I was young
That I had been a lad,
And learnt to do all manly things
So I could help my dad.
But I am very glad by now
It never came to pass,
I feel so proud and honoured
That I was born a lass.

Just think of all I would have missed,
The catalogue is vast,
Remembering all the things that fill
The memories of the past.
My female friends, the fashioned clothes,
The shoes that were in style,
The hair and make-up to entice,
Shy boys that ran a mile.

The way I blushed when I first met
He who would pass the test,
To share the privilege to love
The baby at my breast.
The saying is the hand that rocks
The cradle rules the world,
I quite agree that females all
Are worth their weight in gold.

M E Roberts

GOLDEN YEARS

It seems like only yesterday,
That I wore my wedding gown,
But many years have now passed by,
From the day that the sun shone down.

We've had our ups and had our downs,
Our laughter and our tears,
But now we have reached our golden,
Married for fifty years.

There has been many happy times,
And times of sadness too,
But with grandchildren around us,
There is always plenty to do.

It's hard to believe we have come so far,
How quickly the years have flown,
Now we are just the two of us,
And still plenty to be done.

But we thank God for what we've had,
And take things day by day,
With love and joy and happiness,
A blessing in every way.

Audrey Haggerty

SINGLE MOTHER

The days were endless, the chores never done,
Life lost its meaning, no warmth or fun.
Left alone and afraid, so hard to bear,
Despondent, desperate, no one to care.

One cold frosty night, despair turned to joy,
As I cradled so gently my newborn boy.
A gift, truly precious, beyond compare,
My baby, so trusting, needing my care.

Unfailing devotion became my goal,
As I blossomed in my maternal role.
Committed, dependable, always there,
Imparting my love, giving my care.

Together we flourished, as days turned to years,
Through achievements, defeats, laughter and tears,
To slowly develop the bond we now share,
My reward; a son showing *me* his care.

Claudia Thompson

MEMORY BOX

Clearing away memories that are so old
They smell stale,
He found a carefully hidden box
Made of long summer evenings and rainy school days,
Full of classroom scribbles.

He remembered standing in the cold, damp, yard,
Sharing a soggy cigarette.
Tightly holding her fingers,
Her delicate, milky, frozen fingers
Until he was numb.

Staring at her innocent face
Concentrating on reading a passage from 'Macbeth'.
Mrs Matthews shouting at him
For not paying attention;
Secret smiles.

Anxiously awaiting the echo of the bell
To ring in his ears
So he could run to the school gates
And find her standing there,
Waiting for him.

Carly Hughes

THOUGHTS

When I'm alone, or feel alone,
And cruel words echo around,
My human mind is always there
To shield me from the angry glare.
It gives me hope and lets me see
The wonders that are ours to share.
It helps my humour to return,
And soon the laughter comes again.
It shows me challenges to face,
And knowledge that I need to store.
And life is good and words are kind,
And may it last forever more.

But sometimes a sadness fills my heart,
Weighed down by dreams still unfulfilled.
I miss my loved ones gone before,
And long to hold a grandchild near.
And then my human mind conspires
To lead me to the things I have.
My love of words, the joy of friends,
The care and love my marriage brings.

But my thoughts are mine and mine alone.
They rise unfettered like a bird,
And float above the cruel word.

Janet Tolliday

ALONE WE STAND

Alone we stand in a world
with fear of what's to come.
We fear for our children.

Alone we stand with our heads held high,
for we cannot show our fear
to the children in our world.

Alone we stand with tears that fill our eyes,
but we cannot let them show
for this is our weakness.

Alone we stand with hope in our hearts
that we can help make the world a better place
for our children.

Melanie Trinder

THE IT GIRL

The first thing I saw
when I looked in her eyes
were the lines that were left
from the times when she'd cried.
She says, 'Why does it hurt?
Why do I feel this pain?'
And it's too hard to tell her
We all feel the same
and there's no way of knowing
that there's no way to show
which way she is going
or what she should do.
Deep into her eyes
but the lines are disguised
hidden by hardness
and yesterday's lies.
Yet forever they'll be there
as she laughs at the sun,
at the chances that passed her
and the life that goes on.

Elizabeth Fletcher

DREAM ON!

Sometimes I sit and wonder why
The older I get the time does fly
The days, the weeks, even years
I really could break down in tears
There's never time to sit and think
Or paint my nails pretty pink
To soak in a bath of lovely bubbles
Or chat to friends about our troubles
I think I'd like to take a rest
Just stop the clock, would be best
I'd lay in bed till maybe ten
Soak till eleven, and perhaps then
Phone a friend, chat for an age
Read the paper, page after page
Do my nails and my hair
Dress myself with distinct care
Phone my lover for a late bite
Then back for afternoon delight
Bliss

Trudy Moss-Pearce

MY TEENAGER'S ROOM

Please clean up your room and don't be a slob,
If you do it now it will save me a job.
Look at your clothes all over the place,
Can you not see the untidy disgrace?
CDs and tapes all making a din,
Sweet papers, crisp packets all miss the bin.
Do I see fur growing out of that cup?
Oh! You are a dirty pup.
Just wait till you have teenagers of your own,
Then you'll understand why I did moan.

Margaret Stanley

LUCY

Sleeping child on dream-tossed bed,
I quietly kneel and kiss your head,
Your beauty takes my breath away,
Even after such a day.
You stomped and shouted, played me up,
Then you broke my favourite cup.
What a tyrant you can be,
A screaming witch from purgatory.
Now, eyelashes wet on tear-stained cheek,
In your hand a crumpled sheet.
You look like an angel in repose,
Apple cheeks and cherub nose.
Who would think an hour ago,
All I heard was No. No. No!
You'll wake tomorrow sweet and gentle,
Or do your best to make me mental.
It doesn't matter what you do,
All my life belongs to you.

Felicity Du Valle

SHE-WOLF

Beware the wolf at the door,
If you want to hide
From the truth inside.

She is the path-finder,
The wise one
Who sees your soul.

Love like hers
Can feel terrifying
If you're denying
Who you really are . . .

Caroline Hodgson

HOPE

Cracks in the ceiling
Damp walls all around
Huddled in a corner trying to keep warm
The smell of perspiration through days of wearing the same old clothes
Bony fingers hold a single crust
The only remains of what a pigeon has left

The wind howls
And the rain pours
And still he begs for more

The little cap is empty
No coins have tinkled into its soft material

How long will he sit and beg
And how many people will just walk by

The snow has started to fall
And still he sits
Not moving a muscle
Just waiting for the joyful tinkle
Of coins falling into the soft cap

The light is fading
Doors are being shut and curtains drawn
And still he sits upon the lawn

Morning has dawned
And all that is left of the lonesome figure
Is a frozen statue of poverty on the lawn
And an empty cap waiting to be worn

Zena Samuels

BUTTERFLIES

Butterflies, butterflies,
what an extraordinary name,
for a creature that graces the skies,
full of colour, and no two the same,

Earth's angels, sky's blossoms,
would more suit their grace,
their lives are just so awesome,
the transformation that takes place,

from egg to caterpillar,
but that's not all you see,
they then turn into butterflies,
so beautiful, so free,

such shame, their lives are short,
they seem to savour every second,
fluttering, flower to flower,
wherever they are beckoned,

our life, it also passes,
like the fluttering of wings,
we should visit every flower,
and accomplish many things,

we may then look at ourselves,
with the same wonder and delight,
as when we see a butterfly,
restful from its flight.

Natasha Davies

A CHILD'S CRY - A MOTHER'S NIGHTMARE

I stay in a place that's called Larkhall,
I live there with my little boy,
When he was a tot he broke my heart,
Always wanting to cross to the park.
The swings were just across the road,
He could see them constantly from our abode,
Wait till I finish the dishes, son,
Wait till I hoover the floor,
Our toddlers are much cuter than that,
Turn your back they're off like a flash.
So come on Prime Minister, do your own thing,
And let Britain's children cross safe to the swings.
Make it a law that all must abide,
To have swing parks and pedestrians going along side by side.
Let Great Britain once more rise to fame,
With their children's safety their foremost aim.

Margaret Colville

A WOMAN

A woman is a child, a girl, a lover, a mother.
She'll party with you,
Laugh as the bubbles sparkle and rise in the glass.
Share your passion.
Listen in the dark hours when doubts assail you,
Listen and understand.
The future - the step into the unknown,
'You will succeed. We'll see it through',
A woman copes with life, because she is, a woman.
Remember sometimes,
Bring her roses.

June Holmes

GROWTH AND DECAY

a snowdrop
crumbling flesh
peeping up
peeling away
new grass
receding and regressing
white against green, fresh and clean
old age, middle age, youth and birth
dew and rays of sunlight
layers of skin

shadows from dark-fingered trees, overhanging and menacing
but the stalk keeps pushing up, a David against a Goliath

intense and intent on feeding off the sun, the flower is
suddenly full-blown and standing strong

Mairead Macbeath

LOVE IS

Love is hand held safely in yours.
Love can be friendship, it has no doors.
You can take love or give it, or both if you like.
Love is all around us, daytime or night.
Love is a squeeze when tears make you blind.
Love is a smile when life is unkind.
I've always known love all of my life.
I know about tears and a little of strife.
I found my love in the village one day,
Walking towards me, what would he say?
The village changes little, neither does our love.
Nor do all the stars at night and our Lord above.

Hilda Humphries

Entirely By Woman

Entirely by woman, but not without man,
Has always been God's creative plan.
'I will give you a help meet,' God said one day,
And so with a rib, woman came to stay.
That was a very long time ago, be fruitful
and multiply was the command,
God knew that it was wise to have woman and man.

As years pass by and our family have grown,
Life is not an adventure into the unknown.
As Jesus was man and he died on the tree,
To save us poor sinners that we might be free.
Equality here might be hard to explain,
That would mean Jesus would have died in vain.

Women are mothers and this you can see,
They do this job splendidly.
In past generations the job was the same,
But men did the jobs like digging the drain.
Man's helping hand will always be good,
He is responsible for working for food.
I think you are getting an ache at your ear,
As I make my point loud and clear.

Equality means sameness I know,
But how can this be if God says it's not so?
We think we are clever about making the rules
If our grandmothers were here they would think us as fools.
Active encouragement is a good plan,
Opinions and thoughts still include man.
Can we remember what the good book says?
This is not a woman's world, okay.

Elva Skelton

THE NINTH MONTH

Leaves twisting, turning, bonfires burning,
Conkers falling to the ground.
Squirrels scamper, there are many
Treasures it seems to be found.

Morning misty, evening darker.
Acorns scattered - now many more.
Trees are barer, looking starker,
Planting seeds on an autumn floor.

Ochres, russets, yellows and reds,
Another season nearly done.
How quickly the leaves from trees are shed,
As autumn and winter merge as one.

And yet each year I still enjoy,
Scrunching leaf mould under my feet.
Blackberries, mushrooms - join the foray
These woodland prizes taste so sweet.

Nights are longer and much colder,
Frosts appearing on my windows.
Another season and one year older
It's time to dress in warmer clothes.

Welcome winter and a new season,
But may the next nine months quickly pass
For I have the best of reasons -
Another autumn, long may it last.

Heather J Allsopp

A Bed

A bed is a bed is a bed
A place to rest your weary head
A 'Shaky-doon' I don't want to remember
Was my bed one night in December.

The water pump had gone caphoot,
The central heating up the spoot.
So a 'Shaky-doon' for me -
The boiling water to release you see.

The chairs, one fireside, one easy,
A couple of bottles to make life easy.
The chairs together, blankets round,
Then the draughts soon are found.

Settled at last,
Ten minutes flat
When the pipes start
Their rat-a-tat-tat!

The water steaming down the drain,
This is causing my great pain.
Back to the 'Shaky-doon' I go
One bottle cold, the other empty,
Well maybe I've had plenty.

The night is full of ups and downs,
The morning sees me with a frown.
The plumber comes and puts things right
Oh great, I'll get to my bed tonight.

As I lay down my weary head
I thought:

A bed is a *bed is a bed!*

Muriel E MacKay

HOW MY LIFE HAS CHANGED

I was born into this world a daughter,
Later to become a sister,
Grew into a young woman,
And went looking for a mister!

At the age of eighteen
I pledged my troth and became a wife,
To have and to hold
For the rest of my life.

Three years wed and my life changed again,
As into this world a daughter came,
As friends for life we would remain,
You will always be a daughter and friend to me.

Three years on a son was born,
Is it possible to love another?
Here I am a wife and mother,
Have I lost my identity?
What has happened to me?

Back to work I go,
Now I am me, not a mother or a wife,
Still ready to let the love and support flow,
Nothing would I change as you are all my life.

For I am the richer you see
For having a wonderful family
Who really mean the world to me,
For without you all, where would I be?

June Toms

YOU

Every time I think of you, there's hope
And an assurance that I can win.
Your face is etched in my mind
And your wholeness fills my empty heart.
The anticipation of what might be makes me thirsty,
Hungry to know more of you.
You are so different to the rest
Unique in your attraction
Familiar, yet unknown
Confident, yet unsure.
Your strength empowers me
And your warmth renews me
Each time you are here.
I will try because you believe I can.

Rachael Parker

LOVING YOU FROM AFAR

Watching you every day,
Sleeping, speaking, every way,
Listening and watching
Is all I can do.
Just waiting for a sign,
A sign from you.
Loving and feeling
The way I do,
Just makes me want
To kiss and cuddle you.
Eyes tell a lot
Or so I am told,
So show me your eyes
And let the truth be known.

Paula Snowdon

UNTITLED

I get up in the morning
and then I never stop,
from washing, ironing, cleaning
and dashing to the shop!
I have to get home 'pronto' -
collect my son from school,
I'm at the gates at half-past two
and don't I feel a fool!
The time goes by so speedily
I'm bound to get it wrong,
so then I quietly shunter off
to home - where I belong!
So many things to do each day
one day rolls into two,
we're women in this modern world,
there's me and also you.

L Buxton

OMELETTE METAPHOR SCRAMBLED (HAIKU)

Those eggs you have taken
And broken and beat
Were all from my basket.

Rebecca Hayward

LOVE POEM I

You are my mother
I loved you
I revered you
Looked up to you
Followed you
And copied you
Warm, wholesome
Encouraging
And constant
You are my mother

You are my mother
In love
With the family
In love
With the home
And garden
Changing beds
Cooking in the kitchen
Washing on the line
In love
With the simple life
You are my mother

You are my mother
A gentle rock
A heart of wisdom
A seeking soul
Carrying a light
Yet searching load
Guiding, demonstrating
Winsome and shy
You are my mother

Margaret Bennett

Papa Freud's Pieta

Afraid, we lurked in the hayloft, our home,
reached only by a broken ladder:
precarious safety of the sky.

In the coral below raged
the magnificent red bull
whose littleness in pity we had
once taken in, my sisters and I.

And my growing child could not
touch earth, without risking his life:
the dark madness in those eyes
waited only for his eager, uncertain step.

In the heat of the afternoon
they caught him, his raging encircled
by blue jeans and leather hats
calling and laughing, while the pounding hooves
trampled the silent and wounded earth.

But his death would be mine:
the kitchen knife leapt to my hungry hand
and my feet flew thirstily down the broken steps.

At sunset that knife
found a heart.

But the ribs it had broken
were the ribs
of my child.

Gisela Hoyle

SUBMISSIONS INVITED
SOMETHING FOR EVERYONE

POETRY NOW 2003 - Any subject, any style, any time.

WOMENSWORDS 2003 - Strictly women, have your say the female way!

STRONGWORDS 2003 - Warning! Opinionated and have strong views. (Not for the faint-hearted)

All poems no longer than 30 lines.
Always welcome! No fee!
Cash Prizes to be won!

Mark your envelope (*eg Poetry Now*) *2003*
Send to:
Forward Press Ltd
Remus House, Coltsfoot Drive,
Woodston,
Peterborough, PE2 9JX

**OVER £10,000 POETRY PRIZES
TO BE WON!**

Judging will take place in October 2003